Perf

Perf

THE UNSPOKEN FLAWS IN A "PERFECT" CULTURE

CHLOE CULLEN

NEW DEGREE PRESS

Perf
The Unspoken Flaws in a "Perfect" Culture

ISBN   978-1-63676-481-8   *Paperback*
       978-1-63730-385-6   *Kindle Ebook*
       978-1-63730-386-3   *Ebook*

CONTENTS

———

This is the mark of perfection of character—to spend each day as if it were your last, without frenzy, laziness, or any pretending.

—MARCUS AURELIUS, *MEDITATIONS*

Researchers can argue back and forth about whether or not an adaptive form of perfectionism exists, but colloquially, how bad off are you if your disorder can be preeningly confessed? A leper can't say I'm such a leper... perfectionism's rep as ambition on steroids remains glossy: it can present not as delusion, but as an advantageous form of sanity.

—ELIZABETH TALLENT, *SCRATCHED: A MEMOIR OF PERFECTIONISM*

For some reason I had this idea that I was really special and that I was put here to do something really great and important, but the longer I kept living the more it just seemed like nope, I'm just kind of a normal person just like everybody else.

—RAPHAEL BOB-WAKSBERG'S SHORT STORY "UP-AND-COMERS"

INTRODUCTION

———

"I never did drugs in my life. I never smoked. I don't drink, I never had a cup of coffee, I don't drink soda. I just don't go near any of those things, but my drug of choice, my favorite drug, is winning," Dan Pope told me. "Winning is my favorite drug."

Daniel Pope Karate Institute outside of Philadelphia convinces newcomers of its success with trophies. They line the glass walls facing out onto the street, some with heights ranging higher than Pope's six-foot posture, and they occupy any available table space in his office. Each trophy Pope won himself.

Since he started his career at fifteen with martial arts and karate competitions, he established a routine. In the arena, he approached the trophy and stared at it before retreating to a back, private room. He lay down and prayed as he visualized how he would, God willing, win the competition with each step he took leading to the victory, from the breakfast he ate to the sweatpants he wore to the roundhouse kicks he would deliver to beat his opponent.

And Pope won. A lot. He appeared in local magazine articles and televised features, and he opened the Daniel Pope

Karate Institute with his winning reputation as the main advertisement. (He is quick to point out that his studio has outlived many neighboring karate studios that have opened and closed in his studio's tenure.) The winning brought success, but the losing was unbearable.

"I took losing as if it was a death," Pope said. "I cried. I was depressed. It could kill me. I wasn't your typical athlete. I left everything I had in the arena, and even leading up to it, my practices were do or die. My thinking, my eating, my sleeping, my vitamins, everything was to win at all costs."

Though retired after a twenty-five-year career, Pope still seeks to win at any aspect of life. He drafted a team for August practices to win at his church's Thanksgiving pickup football game. (He won a spot in the church's Hall of Fame, which he founded.) He learned how to play the violin as an adult and not only plays now but also chased this curiosity into the chance to hold $7 million worth of violins—just to know how it felt to hold them. For Halloween parties, he has spent more money on pirate costumes than the prize money for the costume contest itself (which he won). He has written three books, visited the Cody Firearms Museum archives to hold rifles that belonged to famous gunslingers like Wild Bill Hickok and Annie Oakley, and stared down grizzly bears in Alaska.

Even in leisure, Pope strives to be the best. If he wanted to golf, for example, he wouldn't take lessons from a local pro at a Philadelphia course; he would golf with Tiger Woods on the best course in Scotland. "I will go to extreme levels, eccentric levels, to accomplish what I'm looking for," Pope said. "I just can't settle for the mundane, the norm. I got to experience something at a high level."

Though he checks his perfectionism through his Christianity, he cannot understand why his kids or pupils ever place less than their full potential into any effort. "If they don't want to go to the levels I did want to go to, then I don't understand it. It's almost as if you started speaking Russian right now," Pope said. "If you're playing a guitar and you're not putting three hours in, I don't get it. If you're playing basketball, and you don't take 100 and something shots a day, I don't get it. I really don't. I'm not kidding. I don't get it. Matter of fact, I get mad about it. Yeah, because I think wasted potential is a horrible thing."

Dan Pope is, on paper, the perfect perfectionist. He has gained success in his field and turned his passion into a living. His work ethic is as gold-standard as his trophies. His success allows him to explore his interests at the highest level of curiosity and expertise.

As my first book interview, he can't tell that at this point that I consider myself, and all those days I couldn't bring myself to write, wasted potential. A failing perfectionist.

It is November of the pandemic. The leaves continue to change as if the world is the same as it was the year before. I teeter consistently on the edge of existential angst. Whoever I am with, whether it's my grandma or my boyfriend or my parents, I am not really there. A looping, warped vinyl runs in my head that says, *You should be writing. When are you going to write today? Are you going to put it off again? You're a fake.* Whenever I schedule time to write, I freeze and distract myself with exercise or errands. Other people on Instagram post homemade sketches or poetry. Everyone successful seems to be younger than me; at twenty-five, I feel closer to the "Aunt Chloe" label that my younger sisters have (jokingly) given me. Instead of buckling down on my own habits (or lack thereof), I fume other people are getting ahead in creating content.

Instead of unpacking my disgust at my discipline (and then my frustration at my disgust), I wanted to discover why millennials and Gen Z kids all sought passion and fame. I wanted to know why we fought so hard to be remembered through what we made. I wanted an answer for how we should be living. I wanted to know that, by the end of my life, I will have done something successful and meaningful, and I wanted this book to tell me how to do it.

Someone must have the answers for a perfect life.

At the end of our interview, Dan Pope asked me, "Is this a good interview? Are you getting what you're looking for?" He confessed he wanted to be the most perfect perfectionist that I researched. Maybe, I thought, we both are still searching.

I told him yes, as if I knew.

**

Living in Los Angeles came with its benefits: the sixty-degree weather in February, the mountains and beaches, the buzz of new industry slang and intel from my own lips, a comedy exposure through a theater internship that granted me free access to all theater shows. I attended five or eight shows a week, sometimes back-to-back, then I wrote reviews for my boss to analyze potential talent. Though I spent most of my time writing coverage on other comedians' web series or live shows, I silently considered myself better, funnier, sharper with no materials of my own to prove my hypothesis. I thought I had the *it factor* that everyone else on stage or in the constant rotation of improv classes sought for themselves.

In the last week of my internship, my boss arranged exit interviews to see how she could help me and the other interns with our next career move. In that windowless, incense-filled room, my boss looked at me across her small desk. Her large foster dog snored next to her. When she asked what I wanted to do, I said, "I think I want to be a writer—"

"You can't think," my boss interrupted, "that you want to be a writer. You have to know it. If you say, 'I think,' then you don't really want it because it's hard work. The people who know they want to be writers work five hours every day, and they still might not make it."

I nodded.

Maybe I had been wrong about my potential.

What, Chloe, you thought that your time at a comedy internship gave you a funny badge? Chloe, you expect everything handed to you. You never work for anything. All those LA people you met never questioned their own accomplishments. And you think you can write when people want it more than you do. You're a fake. And you're not a writer.

Since that spring three years ago, my self-doubt and entitlement have shifted in waves. One day, I will revise an old short story and tell myself that I'm great. The next day, those same pages will reek of sentimentality. The day after that, I tell myself that I missed my chance. If I really was any good at anything, someone would've noticed by now, or I would've put something out there that had gone viral, or I wouldn't have to try so hard to get myself to just sit down and write.

As Americans, we believe in climbing the ladder, spitting the tooth in tough times, and reaching the top. It's as foundational to our identity as the Founding Fathers, who also lived by this model for democracy. If you are good at something with that hybrid mix of natural talent and endless work ethic, we believe recognition and awards will find you.

As Elizabeth Gilbert said in conversation with Suleika Jaouad,

The cultural message in the capitalistic, Protestant work ethic society is that you—let me know if this narrative sounds familiar—you all have one gift that you are given by the universe within you. And your job in life is to find out what that gift is, and then to cultivate it, and then to become the master of it, and then to become the best of it out of anyone in the world, and then to monetize it, and then to become really successful at it, and then to expand it so other people can be included and their lives can be changed by it. No pressure, but that's the fucking brief.

Perfectionism refracts unrealistic expectations from every angle of my life. *You're too old to only know how to boil noodles and eggs. You still need to watch the Oscar-bait films from 2018. You have to prove you're smart since you didn't go to an Ivy League school. If you worked harder, you would be making more than minimum wage. You don't reach out enough to your friends. You only talk about yourself. You need to be less selfish. You need to volunteer more.*

Perfectionism is an idea that is honored, despite our outspoken acceptance that perfection doesn't exist. Though perfectionism has a type-A connotation—a fastidious eye for otherwise unseen details—perfectionism relies on transactional conformity. A perfectionist focuses on the details to be the best. Barbara Streisand, for example, calls herself a perfectionist. However, the attempt to be the best, even for an icon like Barbara Streisand, requires becoming "the best" to other people. It hinges on acquiring the affirmation of others and staying likeable to a universal and faceless population. It means there can be no mistakes, no flops, no failures—even if those failures come through in the details no one else sees.

Though perfectionism plays for the appeal of a mass audience, everyone's idea of "perfect" is subjectively fluid. Despite clichés like "if we were all perfect, life would be boring," we strive for a personal variation of perfection. Your idea of a perfect partner, a perfect career, or a perfect self will differ from my idea of my desired perfection, but the individualized expectations of perfection seek to transform us from an ambitious, Frankenstein-ed version of ourselves. Be as funny as that comedian, as intellectual and well-spoken as a *New York Times* writer, as selfless as your mother—or Mother Teresa. Sure, we can't be perfect, but we can be smarter, prettier, funnier, or any other improvement based on the people around us who seem to be effortlessly smarter, prettier, funnier, etc.

With this desire to mold ourselves to evolving standards, perfectionism can be toxic. Dr. Keith Gaynor in his talk "Why Perfectionists Become Depressed" discusses the cycle of low self-esteem through high expectations. Take an employee whose goal is to meet their quarterly target. The employee can either (A) meet the quarterly target, (B) miss the quarterly target, or (C) avoid working toward the target at all. In option C, the employee who doesn't do the work and "fails" is still a perfectionist. Welcome to the procrastination pillar of perfectionism. This employee tells themselves they will never do the job perfectly, so they don't do the job at all. This may surprise our normal idea of perfectionism.

What is more surprising is the ideal worker in option A will not see themselves as accomplished. They rationalize their work as ordinary or even subpar by telling themselves and others, "Anyone can meet the quarterly goal, everyone else did, it's not a big deal."

As it becomes easier to compare ourselves to our icons and our peers through social media or a Siri search, it's easy to have someone on that internal corkboard of "perfect" to incentivize improvement. As a result, whether the perfectionist chooses option A, B, or C, it results in the same low self-esteem for all three employees.

If we don't know how to dismantle the reinforced and painful process behind our motivation, we will find ourselves stuck in the same unsatisfied loop through every stage of our lives.

It's easy to be lost in this world that calls us to know our purpose, find our passion, and save the world from climate change, fascism, class inequality, or social injustice. Those issues could sum up 2020 alone. As we already know from various songs or mantras, the only independent variable in life is change.

However, we are desperate for someone else's road map to navigate the right kind of change. We don't trust ourselves to have the answers, so we seek direction. We buy improv classes and self-help books and horoscope apps and Peloton subscriptions for a sense of daily direction. Then we share an abbreviated version of these discoveries through our social media stories. Despite our own indirection, we also want to become surveyors by influence, to reach the top of whatever mountain and yell out our checkpoints to anyone who will listen, perhaps to have them yell back we were right.

Don't get me wrong, I'm on team Learn-From-Others'-Examples. I pour over memoirs and craft books and interviews of people I admire. I also sideline myself by telling myself I don't have all the answers yet. One more article, one more biography, then I'll have the keys, and we can kick it into gear. There is fear in my assumption that I can never make the right choices to find the right answers for myself.

Maybe we all have that fear as the margins for a "perfect life" become narrower, as a life can become quantified by our purchases and possessions.

We breathe in watercolor affirmations like "LIVE. LAUGH. LOVE." or buy expensively bland notebooks embossed with "Dream. Plan. Do." in gold. (Disclaimer: My parents bought me a notebook that says "You got this" one day. I cried. It was a sweet note of support from home, but it also made me feel like I had fooled them, because I didn't feel like I got this at all.)

We seek out numbers to score our worth. We shop for bargains, count calories on no-carb diets, subscribe to Masterclass and take a class or two (though there will always be more classes and less time to take them). We build lists of what we want to watch or read versus what we have already consumed. We have likes and retweets. We count daily streaks on wellness apps for exercise or meditations. We add up our salaries and the bills, and any tightness between what we owe and what we earned can feel like a personal character trait.

We face endless questions in our everyday lives, ranging from the nightly navigation through the quicksand of Netflix's library to silently Googling "purpose how find" or "ocean spray skateboard man why trending."

In a world of quick yeses—viral growth of likes and retweets, or the "yes" to let Netflix know you are still watching four hours later—the short-term yes is productive. Certain agreements can craft a positive path to a job offer or a Zoom happy hour or even a morning walk, but it is easy to procrastinate the long-term focus with an easy yes. An easy yes to another episode of *Love Island UK* delays the long-term questions that do not have yes or no answers, like "When does my unemployment benefit run out?" or "How long before my biological eggs turn to dust?" or "How will I know when I'm at my peak of happiness or if I've passed it?"

Having a consumable yes available satiates our need for control. That productivity of one yes vibrates like a twenty-first century adult Bop-It: Prime it, binge it, tweet it, scroll it, awwwwh! Yet for all the affirmation, Americans, especially millennials and Gen Z, face rising rates of depression and anxiety. The Pew Research Center found that seventy percent of Gen Z survey participants found anxiety and depression as a problem among their peers, and a 2019 Blue Cross Blue Shield study found that millennials' physical and mental health deteriorates faster than Gen X adults did at the same age.

I can't provide you with answers. I'm not a therapist. I go to one. This isn't a self-help book that claims to bring new light to your daily life. I don't have a formula to say this is the way to combat your perfectionism. I can't give you that long-term answer that would end that nagging indecision and deliver you eternal calm, but I can tell you what I was thinking as I learned my perfectionism was not helping me.

Consider this a book of short explorations into culture that I never considered before. Consider it as short streams of consciousness around things I like that also reflect my perfectionist lens these past twenty-five years. Consider these questions that I considered when I started writing:

- What makes a pop star?
- Why did *Hamilton* pop off so much?

- Why did I pay so much for improv classes?
- What is the deal with Martha Stewart?
- How do I become Billie Eilish when I grow up?
- Have I ever stopped to listen to who I actually want to be?
- Or have I assumed I have to be one of the greats to be anything, regardless of whether that's what would bring my life the most satisfaction?

By piecing together cultural fixtures, I will point out the lessons we have gained through cultural osmosis. Pointing it out and naming it hopefully gives you, and me, the power to unshackle the expectations we've carried that weigh us down.

PART 1

"You got to cut yourself some slack.
Cut yourself a break."

—MY PARENTS

CHAPTER 1:

THE POP QUIZ

———

Does looking at a multiple choice structure in an outline give you hives? Do you have slight PTSD from the SAT or GRE or the TerraNova tests you took back in third grade? Then you're the ideal contestant for "What Kind of Perfectionist Are You?" My version of a BuzzFeed quiz that simultaneously feels like a Meyers-Briggs test and an SAT scantron all in one!

So get anxious and tense, because that's the way to take this one! Woo!

Are you a perfectionist?
1. Yes
2. Absolutely not
3. I've never thought about it before, but it could be likely!

I'll let you peek at the answers on this one. The correct answer is (1) **Yes.**

Are you feeling sort of off that I asked your opinion then discarded it?
a. Yes

b. Nah, I'm cool, but like, don't do that again.
c. I'm confused by this lay-out of information.
d. I'm here to have an open mind!
e. I hate this.

Cool, got it! Won't throw you for an emotional loop like that again. But here's the thing. We live in a perfectionist society! Perfectionism manifests individually, but it results from varying societal factors.

If your parents wanted you to be "the best" to make a wonderful future for yourself, you might have worried you had to get good grades or behave correctly in public to appease them. That one-on-one relationship has apparent cause and effect on how perfectionism can become contagious in human dynamics.

A single perfectionist can influence a space, and a perfectionist space can create a perfectionist individual.

For example, that perfectionist parent goes to work. They also want their employees to be "the best" and require flawless work. The stakes appear high because a mistake can translate into dollars or client satisfaction. You can't shrug off mistakes. We must eradicate them to keep things at baseline production. Employees fear mistakes from themselves or others and shame anything sloppy or accidental. It has a trickle-down effect. A boss calls out the flaws of their subordinate, who calls out the flaws of their assistant until everyone is slightly paranoid. What number mistake will it be until they lose the job entirely? Discovering that answer is not as cute as that owl who says, "Let's find out!" about the licks to the center of a Tootsie Pop—though the workplace may be as impatient.

Likewise, let's go back to that student who has a perfectionist parent. It's clear why the one-on-one influence of parent to child would've yielded a mini-perfectionist. The parent wants the kid to go to the best college to have the best career prospects, but the students' friends have that same pressure despite different familial dynamics. These kids have grown up believing if they don't go to college, they won't be successful. The kids are just as scared as their parents about the future. As college acceptances become expected for most, students have to think about how they can be perfect on paper—or at least better than their friends. A bad test could cause tears and catastrophizing that makes the student think they will never get into any college. Those with less advantaged socioeconomic backgrounds are expected to work twice (or three times) as hard to keep up because the expectation of a perfect resume and report card remains the same.

This pressure comes from parents and peers because of the culture we live in. If failure happens, it has to be optimized into a teaching moment that advances the even bigger future success. We live in a mistake-averse zone, and it's contagious. As far as we know, a mistake could cost us a job, financial security, relationships, everything!

Most institutions, from workplaces to education, worry about becoming the best in a hypercompetitive capitalist field. Odds are you are probably a perfectionist by virtue of being alive in perfectionist spaces in 2021, at least in some parts of your life.

Do I still have your attention or are you still mad that I called you a perfectionist?
    a. You don't have to judge me like that.
    b. As individuals, we all have control over our own lives.

c. My perfectionism is actually the reason for all my success.

d. I'm just, like, not a perfectionist.

e. Classic lib millennial blaming society.

f. I could never be mad at you for expanding my horizons!

I hear you. I felt the same way whenever someone told me I was working too hard or being too harsh on myself. (Minus the "lib" dig.) My conversations had never expanded to the societal level because this was a trait I liked about myself. I enjoyed being right that my perfectionism was the right tactic for me. I didn't like someone else talking down to me as if I had broccoli in my teeth my entire life, and they were doing me a favor by pointing it out. *My broccoli was part of my charm! I knew it was there the whole time, but you didn't have to make me feel like it was gross. Don't you dare come near me with that floss!*

In college, my verbal self-criticism induced my then-boyfriend to gift me a book from the checkout section of Urban Outfitters titled *Be Happy!* Out of denial, I never opened the book. Though he wanted to show that he saw me and my depressive symptoms (my constant concerns about being fat or ugly, my stress around my straight A's or extracurriculars), I resented him for thinking something was wrong with me. The book sits somewhere in my parents' basement, suffocating between dusty textbooks.

We tell ourselves perfectionism is our superpower, so if we release our grasp on it, we believe we will become lazy, boring, unmotivated, ordinary. The ground under our feet shakes, and we don't know where we stand anymore.

Still not sold on this whole "perfectionist culture is bad, and we are all perfectionists" thing?
a. No.
b. Learning is the next great adventure!

Okay, then. Do you experience any of the following?
a. You think in all-or-nothing, black-or-white, always-or-never terms.
b. You motivate yourself (or others) through fear.
c. You focus on results over process.
d. You fear failure.
e. You procrastinate.
f. You act defensive.

I would argue that you might've been a little defensive before. Back when I told you that you might have been a perfectionist, and some of you called me a lib millennial? (I know I write the options, but you chose it.)

Back in January 2020, when I had a job and commuted into an office, I browsed James Madison University's website for counseling options. My brother, Collin, was drowning in midterms, and he texted my family that he had barely eaten or slept and was starting to go old-fashioned mad. Being the person I am, a doctor's daughter and a "there's a specialist for that" believer, I jumped to prescribing a specialist for that. While searching JMU's counseling site under the martyrdom of helping Collin, who did not ask for this help, I found a flyer for a JMU clinic called "Reset: Perfectionism."

Do You? it asked,
- *experience intense anxiety, distress, or self-criticism if you make a mistake or do not get a perfect grade?*
- *feel like what you accomplish is never quite good enough?*

- *procrastinate on assignments because they have to be just right?*
- *feel less than others if you do not give more than 100 percent on everything you do?*
- *often feel pressured to meet expectations others have for you?*
- *overcommit yourself because you struggle to say no, fear letting others down, or feel guilty when you have free time?*

I paused and looked over my shoulder to make sure my boss didn't see me reading this, like it was a psychological porno. I reviewed the list again and mentally checked each symptom. I had never seen perfectionism defined in simple bullet points or listed for its flaws.

But tell me who is not *doing this! Is this not how people get things done?* I thought. *Is this suggesting that this is just another thing I have to fix about myself? DAMMIT!*

That should be another symptom: evaluate everything in life, from books to breakfast to virtual errands to the elusive "fun," on an invisible to-do list. The flawlessness search cannot exist without a long checklist of possible solutions for a longer list of flaws.

Why keep your perfectionism in check?
a. I don't know.
b. I think I am doing alright in general.
c. I don't want to worry about this right now.
d. What a thoughtful question! But I don't know.

I hear that, kick that rock down the road! Whatever works, works, right?

On the day that I had signed on to write this book, I told my parents, my roommates, and my boyfriend, Luke. They were all shocked; the decision to write a book had almost no build-up. One day I wasn't writing a book. The next day, I was writing a book. I surprised them at how nonchalant my texts or phone calls were.

"Chloe, that's amazing!" they said.

I countered by telling them it wasn't a real book because, for some reason, it didn't feel real. It was just me. I wasn't some famous writer. It would not be a good book if I wrote it. I was nobody, and nobody would read it.

If you were a real writer, then you would've been published in big magazines and picked up by a big publishing company in the traditional way, and you would've already been discovered, I thought.

That night, instead of brainstorming what the heck this book would be about, or even taking a second to think, *Wow, you are making things happen for yourself, Chloe! This is really cool for you!* I scrolled through pictures from my friend's wedding the previous weekend.

Compared to the bridesmaids and thin-armed girls in the group picture, I looked bulbous and swollen. My roommates said they didn't see that at all, but I saw it. After that, I couldn't trust that they weren't just being nice. Why celebrate myself for doing something unimaginable twenty-four hours earlier when I had so many pieces of myself I wanted to improve, to perfect?

It was midnight. My roommates texted me to say President Trump tested positive for COVID-19. "Check your phone," one of my roommates said through our thin wall. I was sobbing about my weight but concealed it. I jumped between texting my roommates—as a calm, regular person—then jumped back into my texts with Luke—as an angry, defensive scorpion. He said I looked fine in the wedding pictures, and he was more worried about how bitter I had become about my body. I didn't want to hear it. *I have always been harsh on myself. It's how I got anything done, ever. What could he know?*

"I think the goal should be to shift your mind around what you want to consume rather than spring to getting 10 pounds off to feel closer to some false reality of what an 'ideal' body should be," Luke texted me. "I think you're very, very harsh on yourself. Much more so than the truth of it."

"But this time," I texted, "being harsh on myself and thinking I'm overweight was true." I didn't realize I had accidentally confessed something.

"What do you mean?" Luke texted back. "Are you saying you are always harsh on yourself and it's usually not for the truth of your situation, but this time it is?"

I hadn't even realized what I had admitted to—that I had manufactured a harness, untethered by proof, but supported by the corrupt prosecutor of my mind.

Stubbornly, I held onto my theory, blind about how I was sounding to Luke or how I would sound to a third-party. I doubled down, insisting I needed to be this way. I needed this false reality that told me I was too fat without any proof, and I needed to be right about whatever false conclusion I decided. No matter what Luke told me was good about me—my humor, my ambition, my determination, my focus, my healthy body, my brain—I countered to tell him he was wrong. It frustrated him to keep arguing with someone unbound in logic. It got to a point where he started a text saying, "This is going to upset you."

I froze in my bed, staring at the three dots, waiting for the message to come in.

"We are going to have kids someday, and you cannot show this self-deprecation as an example for them," read the text. As you can imagine, that didn't make things better.

I'm fucking great with kids. How could he know? How dare he accuse me of inflicting some sort of mental warfare on my future kids? He does not know what he's talking about. I told him as much because now my anger pivoted away from myself and toward someone else's actions. If he took my perfectionism from me, then where would I stand? I'd have nothing, and it would be all his fault.

By the time I went to sleep, my eyelids looked like pink marshmallows. I gritted my jaw and tried to weep silently so my roommates couldn't hear through the cardboard separating us.

In the morning, Luke sent roses and apologies. I held onto the anger because it anchored the belief that I was right. I Googled "perfectionism mental health," partially to prove him wrong. I wanted so badly to be right. (Welcome to perfectionism 101.) But there was a part of me that was exhausted. For the first time, I was curious enough to see if this was something that could be taken away.

My Google search hit *plenty* of results.

We can dig deeper into Dr. Gaynor's lecture "Why Perfectionists Become Depressed":

Which of the following are short-term repercussions for perfectionism?
  a. Worry
  b. Low mood
  c. Fatigue
  d. Poor sleep habits
  e. Muscle tension

f. Catastrophizing
g. Repeated checking
h. Taking too long to complete a task
i. Being overly thorough
j. Avoidance

For me, this sounded like a regular day at the office—or at my apartment, my parents' house, a random diner, a gas station pit stop, anywhere.

Gaynor expresses that perfectionists live in a paradox: the better they're doing, the worse they feel about it. They lean into "always" and "never" statements to look for absolute answers to life. *I must always be a good parent. I must never be late. I will never be cool enough to talk about TikTok without sounding like I'm forty-six-and-a-half. I have to be everything, or I am nothing.*

A perfectionist believes they can avoid failure to create everything they want for themselves, but failure is inevitable. When that failure comes, the perfectionist cannot rebound and will self-criticize, whether the failure was within their control or not.

"What if we engaged in flexible standards?" Dr. Gaynor says. "What would they be like? What would we prioritize if our standards were flexible and open? I like to be a good person most of the time, but it's okay if I lose my temper. I'd like to work hard, but every now and again, I'm going to be lazy."

If a person thinks in all-or-nothing terms, how can they know when they've been too lazy or too bad? The only way to gauge their actions is by shooting for the extremes in order to confirm yes, they are undoubtedly good or hardworking.

Tangential question: What gives you confidence?

a. Positive feedback from an instructor or supervisor.
b. Compliments from a friend.
c. Attention from a really hot person!
d. Purchases that guarantee I look and feel hot!
e. Good report card or GPA.
f. Social media metrics (likes, retweets, etc.).
g. None of the above.

Though everyone has their own things that bring them joy, and no one can determine that but you, I'm grading this quiz and believe that **(g) none of the above** is the healthiest answer based on Dr. Gaynor's lecture.

When perfectionists self-criticize, they cannot point out to themselves when they are doing something well. Therefore, they rely on the validation of other people and things to tell them they are right. If we look at the wedding example again, I tried on multiple dresses in front of friends and asked their opinions on which one I should wear. I chose the one that they liked most on me, because I couldn't trust that my opinion of the dress I liked was correct, that the dress was pretty or flattering. I can walk out feeling confident because a crowd has affirmed my choice. Contrarily, if they didn't like either of my dresses, I wouldn't have felt confident in either of the dresses I chose, though I liked both enough to pack them.

Dr. Gaynor introduces the concept of "swing confidence." Perfectionists, as a result of self-criticism, allow their confidence to fluctuate with external factors. If they do well on a test or get a promotion or receive attention from a cute human, their confidence is high. They believe they have evidence that they are smart, hardworking, or attractive. That confidence crumbles either in the absence of those reinforced compliments or presence of criticism, rejection, or failure.

The healthier alternative, though it isn't easy, is "core confidence," an internal self-assessment that sees the greatness in a person's own strengths *and* weaknesses.

To quote one of Dr. Gaynor's slides, people develop self-criticism origins from times in our lives when others have been critical of us, such as,

- early life experience: coaches, teachers, parents
- gold stars for good work/hard work
- medals for achievement

What other mental illnesses can perfectionism play a risk into?

a. High functioning anxiety
b. Depression
c. Anorexia
d. Bulimia
e. Self-harm
f. Suicidal ideation

With the negative feedback loop of perfectionism, there is always compounding self-criticism. Even when you achieve a goal, it's not enough. It's easy, in that light, to imagine how perfectionist thinking plays into any of these mental illnesses.

Does some of that resonate?

a. I'm with you!
b. Maybe a little.
c. Never!

Based on your experience, which definition of perfectionism is true?

a. I aim to be perfect in everything I do.

b. I have high expectations for the people who are important to me.

c. My social circles (family/friends/co-workers) expect me to be perfect.

If you answered **(a)**, then you are a *self-oriented perfectionist*.

If you answered **(b)**, then you are *an other-oriented perfectionist*.

If you answered **(c)**, then you are *a socially prescribed perfectionist*.

Yay! Wasn't that fun?

According to *Psychology Today*, these three branches distinguish perfectionism. Researchers Paul Hewitt and Gordon Flett created a multidimensional scale for perfectionism in 1991 that discovered these three origins. The answers listed above come from the original study they used to test the varying levels of self-oriented, others-oriented, and socially prescribed perfectionism, ranked on a one-to-seven scale, in psychiatric patients.

However, Hewitt had studied this in college students as well. He told Christie Aschwanden about one of his University of British Columbia students. Hewitt and the student worked toward getting the student an A+ in Hewitt's class. By the end of the semester, the student received the perfect grade but had begun having suicidal thoughts. "I got the A+, but all it did was demonstrate to me that if I was really smart, I wouldn't have had to work so hard to get it," the student said.

"Striving for perfection isn't the same as being competitive or aiming for excellence, which can be healthy things. What makes perfectionism toxic is that you're holding yourself to an impossible standard that can never be achieved—essentially setting yourself up for perpetual failure," Aschwanden writes.

So, is this perfectionism thing losing its luster?
a. Yes.
b. I'm a little scared.
c. I'm a perfect perfectionist!
d. Learning is the next great adventure, so no!

Okay. Are we ready to go back to the societal level yet?
a. You're going to go there anyway.
b. I'm ready for it!

Indeed. What are the societal factors that play into a perfectionism culture?
a. Loserhood.
b. The participation trophy thing that happened to millennials and made them soft.
c. The rise in all men thinking they can do stand-up comedy.
d. The never-ending scroll of Instagram stories.

Yes, to some of those? Maybe those are all different parts of the same answer: we want to stand out but don't want to be left behind.

A common phrase that came up in my research was "keeping up with the Joneses" from the 1950s consumerist, suburban angst of comparing yards and driveways to maintain appearances with neighbors. Now, with social media, anyone can be the seemingly perfect Jones to beat. Instead of competing to own the same new kitchen appliances as our neighbors, we can compare any facet of ourselves to someone better. Think you're funny? You follow a famous comedian who seems more effortlessly funny. Think you're buff? There's a bodybuilder in your feed. Think you're smart? Here are five current events, topics, life hacks, or horoscopes that prove you know nothing.

But can social media take all the blame?

We work in a capitalistic society where people can equate all employees to statistics without appreciating them as individuals. This creates a certain fear to be perfect to continue cogging the larger machine. Newer entries to the workforce are more vulnerable to withstanding overwork because they have to pay off their ginormous student loans. These people have entered the workforce at a time where there is no roadmap and no answers for anyone after roughly twelve to sixteen years of memorizing the right and wrong answers to tests. From a young age, we train ourselves to have the right answers. The good grades were a consequence in the aggressive studying we thought would result in more doors and options in our futures.

I know, I said "capitalism," and some of you are probably nervous. (I can almost hear a faint stubborn yell of "I was right, she's a lib" from the back row of my brain.)

We break our lives into quantitative and qualitative metrics—standardized test scores, salaries, brand-name companies, follower ratios, Tinder matches, Peloton badges, overtime hours, number of side hustle products sold/accepted/published. We can compare all this to other people to determine, in numbers, where we rank in the world.

All of this self-measurement compounded during a pandemic that has cost lives and livelihoods. Some of us (me) are still looking for *something* to do to make the most use of this time and ignore the ingested trauma and threat of constant productivity.

If we ever felt defensive about holding onto a constant and avoiding change, this would be a very difficult year.

So, in this hellish landscape of the world, why let go of perfectionism? What is the benefit of not being a perfectionist anymore?

1. Focus on what you individually need instead of considering everyone else's opinions on what you need.
2. Step out of your comfort zone to discover what you *actually* want to do outside the cookie cutter mold of a life we have digested.
3. Take creative risks.
4. Find out where your interests take you to step into a life that makes you uniquely content.
5. Forgive and empathize with people around you instead of hating them for not living up to your standards.
6. Give your time more happily to others and your community.
7. Appreciate the weirdness in people you love and people you don't know.
8. Make your own metrics for the life you want.
9. Learn to accept change.

Dr. Thomas Curran is an associate professor at the London School of Economics who studies perfectionism. He was also one of the top hits I found in my perfectionist-fueled haze to discover if perfectionism was actually bad. His TED Talk connects perfectionism to society—to a post-Reagan and post-Thatcher world oriented around metrics.

When we spoke, he talked about his grandfather, a carpenter. "I look back, and I'm jealous," Dr. Curran said. "He could make a pub rail, do something for someone else, and finish it. He didn't have to think about it again once he was done." His grandfather could help the community and put work into the world, with his contribution being nearly invisible to the everyday patron.

But now, we live in an age where a carpenter would have to finish the product as quickly as possible, photograph and market the final product, then stress about the next job that may or may not come if the carpenter doesn't hustle.

When I interviewed Dr. Curran early in 2021 with two cats and a dog walking into my Zoom frame, all my questions circled around how someone could fix their perfectionism, extract it from themselves.

I asked:

a. But perfectionism itself is not considered a mental illness itself, or is it?

b. Is there a good perfectionist? Is there someone who just works hard and is not a perfectionist?

c. Or are there ways to readapt your perfectionism to get to that internal completeness?

d. Is there any way we can get to embody your grandpa's mindset now?

And the answer is essentially, no.

Dr. Curran laughed. "If he lived now, he would be a perfectionist, too!"

What I wanted was an answer. How do I cure myself of this? How do I isolate myself from my perfectionism?

The answer is that I can't because perfectionism is a cultural cornerstone for us.

"There is hope," Dr. Curran said. "I don't want to sound too dark, but there is hope. If we can accept failure for what it is, and that doesn't mean thinking about using failure as a stepping stone to success, then we will be in a much better place. If we can accept failure for what it is, there is hope."

That's when I finally got it.

I will never be able to overcome my perfectionism. Not completely.

However, even if I always carry my perfectionism, I can address it and recognize it not as truth but as a string of thoughts that stem from my fears. *What if I'm overweight, not funny, unaccomplished? Will people like me? Will I be alone?* Recognizing these thoughts then putting them away, like a celebrity lap dog from the early 2000s, can give my brain space.

Well, are you ready to read?
a. I'm mostly scared.
b. Does this mean I'm a...perfectionist?
c. Great, one more thing to work out in therapy.
d. Thanks a lot, lib.
e. WAHOO!

Sounds about right.

You have passed the quiz, but you were always going to pass. And perhaps that's the lesson of it—you, as you are right now, pass without having to earn it.

CHAPTER 2:

THE PERFECTIONISM PENDULUM

———

"If this short film isn't so incredibly good, if it is not so incredibly perfect that it gets in all the film festivals in the world, I'll never have a job as a director ever. And maybe that's not true, but at the end of the day it's hard for me to convince myself otherwise," Adam Gherleter said.

Adam recently graduated from a film program in Georgia, works at an established production company where he reviews and writes scripts, and is re-shooting and revising a short film for the film festival circuit. The short film originated as his senior thesis, but that doesn't reflect Adam's ambitions. A student on his thesis shoot said that they could take it easy since this was only a student film. "Don't you ever fucking say that, or I'll kick you off the set," Adam responded.

"It sounds crazy," Adam told me. "I sound like an asshole, but I'm just like, why? Why would you do anything half-assed?"

Adam does not know how to half-ass. In our conversation, he's lively with movie allusions, personal entertainment industry anecdotes, screenwriting reference-text references, and lessons. He talked about how a professor compared budding screenwriters to his potty-trained daughter: making a finished product does not disqualify it as crap. Adam applies the same tenacity to his art. "If I'm going to do something I'm passionate about, I'm going to do that but I'm going to do it right, so I put so much heart and soul into it," Adam said.

For the thesis project, he made a GoFundMe and invested his personal money for a $6,000 shoot with a forty-person crew taking place over six days and two weekends in March 2020. Then he reviewed the footage from the shoot. "And it was horrible," Adam said. He refuses to release even a trailer.

Adam has spent his free time studying how to resuscitate the short for another upcoming shoot. He has rewritten the short script (a typical short script can range from five to twenty pages) over fifty times. He hosted focus groups that talked about the lack of empathy for his protagonist and of inciting incidents. He applied the techniques from screenwriting books and triple-checked to avoid clichés and tropes.

"It's been absolutely consuming my mind, you know," Adam said. "Is this actually getting better, or am I just overdoing it?"

There can always be something else to fix. This is true of anything, but it's especially true with creative projects. When working alone, writers don't have a green light for when character development or plot twists officially work. Sometimes, one friend likes it, and another opposes the feedback you received. Sometimes, everyone has the same critique.

In writing my own stories or chapters, I have relied on other people's guidance more than my own: is this a story worth reading at all? While writing my graduate thesis of short stories and personal essays, my edits became so tedious—for example, a semi-colon to two separate sentences, a verb change, and an additional sentence to describe grass— that my thesis adviser requested that I bold-face any changes so he could spot them in a mostly unchanged manuscript. I tweaked characters. I moved beginning sections to the end. I did this to my thesis adviser multiple times a week. Still, in the post-graduate world when I sent these stories out to magazines, the rejection letters kindly pointed out that there wasn't much action to the stories. All of this to say, I could stare at my own stories letter by letter, but I still couldn't figure out how to make them *work,* and if I couldn't see that there wasn't any plot, how could I trust myself to write anything?

Adam faced this on his own set; some people on set advised he not shoot one scene. He took their advice. In the editing process, this un-shot scene proved to be the climax. The short was incomplete without it. He let his crew's guidance obstruct his view; because once entangled in analyzing each detail, Adam could find a borderline relief and trust in any outside perspective.

Now, Adam is about to reshoot his short, financed again with his own money. He plans to edit the script until the last minute his producer asks for it. "It's definitely going to change because I'm going to read it next week and want to change it again," Adam said.

As discussed in the Pop Quiz, perfectionism creates a swing confidence. A perfectionist's confidence peaks or valleys based on praise or criticism. What individuals need is core confidence, a concrete sense of self that doesn't bend and shake at other people's suggestions. In Adam's case, and in my own, we need to trust our own edits.

In the same way swing confidence can fluctuate, I believe perfectionism can play into two simultaneous extremes: fear and burnout.

FEAR

In high school, Adam played in a band that had recorded an album. It upset Adam that the recording came out "all muddy," and someone told him, "No, it's really good man. It's good enough." "Those words have haunted me for the rest of my life," Adam said. "I absolutely hate the words. Good enough. It just makes me want to scream. It drives me insane. The words 'good enough' are the bane of my existence. I hear it all the time."

Brené Brown's book *The Gifts of Imperfection* roots itself in Brown's research through thousands of interviews to uncover "wholehearted" living. She suggests that the values that we culturally believe will make us the most satisfied— hardworking, put-together, successful—contradicted the traits of people she interviewed who experienced joyful lives.

Brown defines perfectionism as a shield, an addictive belief that convinces us "if we act perfect, look perfect, and live perfect, then we will avoid judgment, shame, and blame." Life guarantees all humans will experience judgment, shame, and blame, but the perfectionist will be doubly upset because they did not "work hard enough" to avoid it from happening. They tell themselves they can avoid future strife if they are more [insert trait here]. Each time the inevitable occurs, and the perfectionist faces distress, they blame themselves for not learning how to avoid it. It is a negatively enforced feedback loop that always seeks more.

We use this perfectionism to find belonging, because we fear that standing out will cause us to be alone. "I'm

convinced that belonging is in our DNA, most likely connected to our most primitive survival instinct," Brown writes.
"Given how difficult it is to cultivate self-acceptance in our
perfectionist society and how our need for belonging is hard-
wired, it's no wonder that we spend our lives trying to fit in
and gain approval."

For me, this can start with something as simple as presents. Around the holidays, my five siblings and I secretly
select one other sibling to buy a present for, and the budget
is $20. It's reasonable considering five out of six kids were
full-time students last year. However, I told myself that my
budget had to be at least $40. (For my financial context: yes, I
had a full-time job, but it was minimum wage in Manhattan.
One of my two monthly paychecks covered rent and just rent.
My parents quietly offered money for me to buy presents. In
short, forty bucks is big spending.) I purchased a wool-lined
corduroy jacket for my brother Collin that I loved. It was
beautiful, but I felt lame to only have one thing for him to
unwrap. *Would this be enough?* No matter how much he said
he liked it, I didn't believe him.

On the flip side, I received a Gryffindor water bottle from
my other brother Carrick. He purchased it on Christmas Eve
from TJ Maxx. I loved this little gift, thoughtful and safely
within my siblings' agreed budget. That cheap water bottle
stayed by my side in my last semester of school. I drank out
of it while teaching and propped it on my nightstand. Its
metal dented and red paint chipped from commuting in my
backpack every day. It became a fixture for me, partially
because I was still bitter that the Harry Potter quiz sorted
me into Hufflepuff. I worried about falling out of Collin's
favor with the present I gave him, but I knew that whatever
my Secret Sibling had given me, I would love.

It's this disconnect in what we can receive and give that makes perfectionism so scary. We allow others the gentle space of being "enough" that we don't give ourselves. We assume our actions risk other people's good-favored acceptance, even for people we love. We will constantly keep working toward their approval, because we cannot accept that there could be a "good enough," so we tell ourselves to push for more or risk losing an abstract yet vital piece of yourself.

That fear of falling below someone's expectations leaks into creativity too. Maybe it's better to put nothing on a page than to put something terrible. Perfectionists paralyze themselves, thinking a mistake means irrevocable loss. Adam believes that this one short determines his career as a director: "At the end of the day, it's hard for me to convince myself otherwise." One short film rarely launches a lifelong career—but it could. The pressure that it could succeed—or crash an early career if the short goes terribly—halts any creative thoughts.

It makes sense why this would apply to a creative person, or to any person who wants to step outside the societal lines written for them. Brown talks about how perfectionism hinders success and creates life-paralysis. "*Life-paralysis* refers to all of the opportunities we miss because we're too afraid to put anything out in the world that could be imperfect. It's also all of the dreams that we don't follow because of our deep fear of failing, making mistakes, and disappointing others," Brown writes. "It's terrifying to risk when you're a perfectionist; your-self-worth is on the line."

Though Brown offers insight into individual behaviors, she calls out "a perfectionist society." It is contagious: "It touches everyone around us. We pass it down to our children, we infect our workplace with impossible expectations, and it's suffocating for our friends and families."

"Perfectionism is that you have to 'do' in order to be loved," Joy R. Berkheimer, a licensed marriage and family therapist, told me. She has treated perfectionism in others and herself by looking at how perfectionism exists on an evolutionary and cultural level alongside the individual's personal experiences.

From an evolutionary perspective, cave dwellers had to blend their identities to match their tribe members for food, shelter, and survival. To step outside the lines meant death. Not the painful social death we fear today. Ate-poison-berries dead. Was-left-behind-for-wolves dead. Our brain uses perfectionism to trigger that same fear of life-and-death whenever we pursue something outside of our comfort zone. "If you don't like me, I am going to perish," Berkheimer summarizes.

This expands out to a cultural level to institutions and societal norms. "If you think of what an institution is, it's a huge tribe," Berkheimer said. What if, she suggested, an employee of a company decided to leave and go backpacking in another country and mentioned it to the CEO and their coworkers? "A group mentality fears the individual," Berkheimer said. "If someone steps out of line, then everyone worries that they are going to fall, or other people in the group will catch the bug about becoming an individual and leaving their role behind." The workers that stay in their cubicles also start to resent the backpacker. Most of them won't follow the individual's example. Instead, they will shape other workers' conformity through gossip or groupthink to make sure everyone else stays in line. The backpacker gets the personalized experience they sought but at the potential cost of their community.

Fear in perfectionism expands beyond simply wondering if your short film or short story is going to fail. It's a constant worry that whatever you do will exile you from our capitalist society. Our capitalist society transacts work for acceptance. Even the fear of failure is enough to guarantee that a typical person works beyond their boundaries for fear they lose their financial stability—and they will keep working until they are burnt-out.

BURNOUT

Rahaf Harfoush lost hair, weight, and sleep before connecting her physical ailments to her mental health. She couldn't think of another idea, which scared her since she had anchored her identity to her productivity. There was no quick remedy for her burnout. "No one loves a good framework or a good acronym better than me," Harfoush said in her TED Talk. However, she discovered her beliefs about her worth had a history in an industrialized workspace.

During the Industrial Revolution, assembly line workers easily measured their productivity. One worker might make fifteen products in a day, and another worker makes ten. They easily translated those measurements to calculate employee performance. "When we shifted to a knowledge economy, people suddenly had tasks that were much more abstract, things like writing, problem-solving or strategizing, tasks that weren't easy to measure," Harfoush said. "We still think of productivity as an endurance sport. You try to churn out as many blog posts, or we cram our day full of meetings. But this model of constant output isn't conducive to creative thought."

Instead of creating new metrics for knowledge-based work, companies instituted the same employee measurement protocols, specifically by measuring employee's effort through timesheets.

Harfoush cites a University of Southern California study that suggests brains actually need time to stop working in order to create new ideas, but this defies the hard work narrative that is embedded into the American identity. A belief as inherent as the American dream—anyone who works hard enough will be successful—suggests that anyone who is unsuccessful is not working hard enough.

Even if an employee answers emails at midnight, takes networking calls to expand their industry knowledge and connections, hosts Zoom happy hours for coworkers, and does some work on Saturday or Sunday to "get ahead" (as Sundays have become pre-Monday in the fluid work from home lifestyle), they might not be picked for the promotion. Why not? Because everyone else in their office is also working that hard, checking emails during dinners, bedtime, or vacations. They work around the clock for fear that no effort they put forward will be enough—to pay the bills, support a family, receive approval from their bosses, feel satisfied.

To circle back to Berkheimer's example, it is more likely that unsatisfied employees will maintain the status quo and critique "the backpacker," or the person who dares to step outside of the implied constant work cycle, for something as simple as taking an impromptu personal day. If an employee carves out time for themselves, the company and its employees might flag that employee as cavalier, and it may risk that person's future in the company. The burnout becomes contagious as everyone fears being the person who is *not* burnt-out.

Once, at my first job, my bosses asked if I could see them in the conference room at lunch. I walked behind them, across the entire floor of cubicles, like a scolded child. They sat me down and told me I had to stop working through my lunch hour.

"There are more mistakes after lunch if you keep working," one of them said. "You need that time to reset."

"And they're not paying you to work that hour," my other boss said gently.

I took this as an insult.

When I first came to this job, one of the assistants— someone that everyone loved for her errorless emails and her friendly demeanor with coworkers and clients—made a throwaway comment about how they're not supposed to work through lunch. "But we all do," she said.

When my bosses pulled me aside to say stop working for free, to the point of careless mistakes like copying the wrong people or sending a client the wrong audition time, I thought it meant I was worse than the other agency assistants.

I stopped working during lunch. If I didn't, my bosses would ask to see when I was stepping away from my desk that afternoon. The days I went to the library branch down the street instead of reading a script and staying on top of emails for dread of whatever might meet me when I clocked back in from lunch, I had a clearer mind. I felt better. I'm lucky my bosses even encouraged the break. However, I still felt there was some shame that I stepped away from my computer while everyone else around me continued to work without being pulled into a conference room.

Keeping our worth in line with our employer's implied or explicit definition allows us to overlook how a perfect employee now involves a twenty-four-hour work schedule. If we value our job, our belonging and stability in a company, more than ourselves, we can never challenge our employers for benefits or higher salaries for fear we might lose everything. This only benefits the companies. Fearful employees won't negotiate their salaries or challenge their supervisors for increased benefits—and no, not benefits like ball pits and all-day cafeterias. Benefits like increased maternity and paternity leave, childcare support, mental health days, and retirement benefits.

Harfoush suggests dismantling our interior thoughts regarding work with questions like "Does being busy make you feel valuable?" Individually, each person will have their own answers to these questions. However, perfectionism allows many people to assume we can control how we are loved by our work. We believe we are what we do. This means we have to maximize our time, even outside of work. For someone like Adam, who pursues his dream of being a director outside of a full-time job, any moment could be an opportunity to learn, network, or create. Not everyone has jobs with fluid work-life boundaries. However, most people feel the pressure today to do more, even in their leisure time.

When I was a kid, my dad stepped out of soccer games, church, and family events to take calls from patients during his turn for the medical on-call rotation. "Be a patent attorney," he told me. "Or a cosmetic dentist. Those guys don't have to get called into work on Christmas or on weekends."

Today, as much as I have gratefully avoided medical professions, I bring my perfectionism to my nine-to-five job and carry that stress with me twenty-four hours a day. I push myself too hard to avoid making mistakes (and carry a light, constant anxiety that a mistake is coming, that I have already messed something up and just don't know it yet). I also bring my perfectionism to my writing outside of work, with pressure on a writing habit or word count quotas every week. I bring my perfectionism to my relationships when I believe I have to do something (plan a trip, buy a coffee) for a family member or friend to earn their love.

This mental struggle to prioritize work in every aspect of our life leads to burnout. It is clearest to spot in a workspace, but the productivity lifestyle—that itch that a perfectionist should do anything other than what they are doing—is fluid and contagious.

Anne Helen Petersen's *Can't Even: How Millennials Became the Burnout Generation* explores all the historical and societal expectation changes that have placed more work, training, and responsibility on employees as millennials have entered the workforce. "Where had I learned to work all the time? School. Why did I work all the time? Because I was terrified of not getting a job. Why have I worked all the time since finding one? Because I'm terrified of losing it, and because my value as a worker and my value as a person have become intractably intertwined," she writes, connecting fear and burnout as two parts of a head-pounding cocktail.

Petersen ties the millennial's strife with their Baby Boomer parents the originators of burnout. As the Baby Boomers entered the job market in the '80s and '90s, their parents called them lazy, entitled, and ungrateful in the same way millennials now face those labels from Baby Boomers. Parents of Baby Boomers, known as the Greatest Generation, had worked at companies that had benefits like social security and Medicaid from President Lyndon B. Johnson's Great Society, but with companies globalizing, profits turned toward the stock markets instead of protecting the employees' benefits.

As the middle-class shrank, Boomer employees feared their financial stability and turned to Reagan, who promised to destroy unions that had popped up to protect the benefits that companies no longer protected. "As boomers were cultivating and optimizing their children for work, they were also further disassembling the sort of societal, economic, and workplace protections that could have made that life possible," Petersen writes.

Millennials raised by Baby Boomers then grew up in Boomer households that encouraged children to go to college and supervised their play from playdates to soccer practice to piano lessons. Millennials then saw themselves as lines on a resume as they entered high school and faced immediate pressure to make that resume, and the quantitative scores of their SATs and GPAs, eligible for the best colleges.

After college, not only did millennials face the 2008 recession in the workplace, but they adapted as their social media and hyper-surveilled lifestyles translated to work. Their hours got longer as they fought to compete with other people over the abstract work they provided. Millennials populated unpaid internships and entry-level jobs and felt the pressure to have a perfect job that was impressive to their parents' friends as well as their peers.

Because these positions have a cool or impressive title, they become a personal identifier that is almost impossible to challenge. Interns are told to work their way up or value the experience that they have, though few students can afford to incur the costs of a daily commute and class credit without compensation. They work more for less security than previous generations, and they believe that their work defines them. They have to think of how their work might lead to something else, something more secure, something that seems to stink less than the opportunity they have now.

"Burnout occurs when the distance between the ideal and the possible lived reality becomes too much to bear," Petersen writes. To paraphrase, burnout happens when we chase an imagined, perfect life that we fear we have to, but won't, earn.

THE CONTINUUM

Earlier in our conversation, Adam mentioned how his choice to pursue a creative career is "that innate, just primate survival instinct that's genetically built into every single human being, to want to live forever."

Nightcrawler, the 2014 Jake Gyllenhaal film about a sociopathic cameraman who sells grisly accident footage to local news stations, plays on this idea. When Gyllenhaal's character, Lou, a literal ambulance chaser, leaves his under-paid intern in the car to trespass and record the aftermath of a triple homicide, the intern gets nervous and leaves the car to catch Lou running from the crime scene. The intern, confused, tries to ask what happened, and Lou yells, "You should have walked in and looked if you're that curious. That's what I'm paying you to do. I need you to show initiative—there is no better way to achieve job security than making yourself indispensable!" The lecture overlaps incoming police sirens.

The desire to be indispensable equates to an irreplaceable quality. "Indispensable" is your grandmother's china and glossy baby photos. As our culture moves toward measuring our worth in productivity, we hope that our work can craft a legacy for us—either creatively or socially. We fool ourselves into thinking that each midnight email or Sunday afternoon on a work laptop clocks time toward becoming indispensable for a company that will ultimately make the financial decision to preserve its own institution—its own legacy.

Indispensable feels like an ideal plateau for a perfectionist work ethic, both safe and secure. Perhaps, if we work hard enough, we will reach a point where we can make time for life. No one would discard us. We can stop working and no one can fire us, lose us, disregard us, ignore us.

A perfectionist, like myself, falls into the belief that their work will outlive them and heirloom a legacy, a story they can control. I didn't see myself working at my first company forever, but I wanted to be indispensable to them, a ghost that would haunt future assistants—"that one Chloe worked through lunch and never complained once." Then I was furloughed during the pandemic. It had nothing to do with whether I worked during lunch. For the company's budget cuts, I was dispensable.

Adam's short is about an older, single physicist who meets a woman online. The date goes awry. The older man replays the date in his head on loop to hope for a different outcome, but no matter what he does, it ends terribly.

When Adam and I talked, I understood him completely. I actually felt relieved to hear another person confirming all of this—the surplus of bad scripts we read when we really want to hear that ours will break the mold if this is the baseline, the constant struggle with a poor-paying job in the hopes of landing somewhere well-paying someday, the pursuit of passion in a world that seems full of passion-chasers. Both of us watched our fathers work tremendously hard and long hours, and we believed we could work the same hours but toward something personally (hopefully) revitalizing. We both hoped that all this hard work, this avoidance of good enough in favor of perfection, would pay off somehow.

Adam is continuing to revise his short film, hoping that it lands some recognition. I edit through this chapter for the fifth time, wondering if it hits the right tone or needs more research. Until we reach this optimistic apex where creativity flows into undisturbed beauty, we will both revise up to the last minute, afraid of what others will say about what we have to say.

CHAPTER 3:

THE INKY FINGER THEORY

"Do you guys remember when I was fifteen, and I fit an entire ukulele head in my mouth?" TikTok user @coochiedestroyer5 speaks to the camera. She rolls her eyes at herself. "Should we see if I should do it again?"

The TikTok cuts to @coochiedestroyer5 after she inhaled a ukulele head, half the silver twists and cord-threaded screws (I clearly never played guitar) hidden in her mouth. The long piece of waxed wood stretches her lips into a six-inch oval and tunnels her mouth away from her chin. She looks like a Tim Burton cartoon in a Star Wars galaxy, assisted by her own shocked eyes above the distortion of her lower face.

Since @coochiedestroyer5 is Billie Eilish, the post has 16.8 million likes and makes headlines.

"Billie Eilish Just Revealed Her Natural Skin Texture on TikTok" is the headline of a *Cosmopolitan* article. "While it's totally up to Billie whether she opts for filters in her videos, I think we can all agree it's so great to see real skin (pores included!) on show—a reminder that everyone's has some sort of texture to it," the article reads.

What struck me about this surreal article is its ending line: "BRB, off to order a ukulele to see if this could be my new party trick too."

It's clearly not the trick that appeals. If I posted that same video, people wouldn't say, "Thank you so much! What a life hack!" The appeal is Billie Eilish, a pop star who breaks the mold with an absurd username and "party trick."

Is the world that obsessed with Billie Eilish that she can do anything for applause? Or is the appeal that Billie doesn't care that she's stepping outside the typical pop star protocol?

Despite her fluidity between genres and labels, between dark and vulnerable, her departure from the norm has built a global fan base and disrupted pop music before her legal adulthood. Her first album, *When We All Fall Asleep, Where Do We Go?* debuted at number one a week after its release, and every song minus the "Goodbye" overture ranked on *Billboard's* Hot 100. The album led her to be the first and youngest to sweep the Grammy's top four awards with Best New Artist, Album of the Year, Record of the Year, and Song of the Year for "Bad Guy" (the "might seduce your dad type" song that somehow tracks behind commercials for pickup trucks, insurance, and meal prep subscriptions). She's been on the cover of *Billboard, Vogue, Elle, Rolling Stone, GQ,* and *Glamour* and endorses designers like Calvin Klein and Gucci with her neon silhouette of form-disguising sweaters and knee-length shorts.

Her dark lyrics and acidic green roots have touched some base nerve of the public, evidenced by the 70.2 million Instagram followers that opt-in for Billie in their hourly scrolls.

I don't know what category you'd put Billie Eilish in, and that's the media narrative around her. "I don't want to be in the pop world," Billie told the *New York Times*. "I don't want to be in the alternative world, or the hip hop world, or the R&B world or whatever, you know? I want it to be…Billie Eilish kind of music. The other kind."

The more she insists she doesn't work in deliberate defiance of the rules, the further the reputation barbs. Jonah Weiner of the *New York Times* wrote in 2020, "NPR called Eilish a 'misfit,' and *Billboard* called her a 'rebel.' *Rolling Stone*, putting her on the cover last July, celebrated her rise as 'the Triumph of the Weird.' When Eilish appeared on the March cover of *Vogue*, the magazine referred to her as 'the Outsider.' Eilish, for her part, does not describe herself, much less seem to see herself, in these terms."

Billie steps so outside the "pop star" box that a new box opens. The rebel. The outlier. The elusive and intoxicating perfume of Billie places her as both aesthetically separate yet emotionally cohesive with her peer group.

Despite the fame, Billie Eilish seems unfazed. She seems happy with her fame and her creative license, as if she, at eighteen, has landed into self-acceptance that no one else in the world finds in their teen years. In short—you know it's coming—she's perfect.

What is the secret? How can I be Billie Eilish?

WHEN WE ALL FALL ASLEEP, WHERE DO WE GO?

Last summer, before the world shut down, my mom gifted me and my sisters tickets to Billie Eilish at The Anthem in Washington, DC. Nothing will quite wake you up to how old you are at twenty-three like waiting ninety minutes in line, sandwiched between pre-teens with clip-in hair color and moms escorting ten-year-old fans.

People were squished together, shoulder to shoulder, by the time we staked out a spot in general admission. To our right, a group of green-haired friends took a picture of their Blotsch tattoos, Billie's icon of a bathroom stick figure shrugging in her signature shoulder shake. To our left, a girl danced alone as her father hypnotized himself with the blue light of his Blackberry's inbox. All of us squished together forty-five minutes before the opener took the stage.

What does Billie Eilish sound like live? I have no idea. The chanting and screaming of her fans overpowered The Anthem's sound system. They knew each lyric. The crowd condensed as people fought for proximity to the stage, the chance to touch Billie's outstretched hand.

What I'm trying to say is that these Billie fans are crazy about Billie.

These fans literally want a piece of her. Billie has had encounters with aggressive fans who won't let go of her hand while she performs, who steal rings off her fingers when she reaches into the crowd, or who wrap their hands around her neck. "She probably didn't mean to because she kind of went like this," Billie told *Vanity Fair* as she shows a hand grazing her chest. "They're only trying to be loving, and sometimes it just comes off wrong."

In the *Vanity Fair* interview, Billie answers the same questions as the 2017, 2018, 2019, and 2020 versions of herself. The 2019 Billie, the green-rooted Billie who opened *SNL* with that glowing skin texture, said, "Success is not how well people know you. It's how you're looked at. I genuinely did not think people would care. I like, can't even stress it enough. I can't believe people care so much about me. It's crazy to me."

I love Billie's music, but I'm obsessed with her calm and certain presence in interviews. I can't even explain it. Amid all the success and disruptions she creates, she seems humble, sharp, and controlled. It amazed her that this has happened to her, but she won't bend to someone else's vision. She seems like someone who knows herself creatively and personally.

Why *do* people care about her so much? Why do *I*, a twenty-five-year-old girl with nothing in common, care about her so much?

Because she has a singular view of the world that taps into the mirrored darkness in the world around her.

Because she's got inky fingers.

WHEN THE PAWN...

A few years ago, on a road trip through a black night, I put on Fiona Apple's 1997 album *When the Pawn…*. My dad, the OG Fiona fan, from the driver seat said, "I always thought Fiona Apple seemed like she had inky fingers. Like she writes so hard her pens break in her hands."

Since that conversation a few years ago, I've thought of that as the parameter for the gifted. The songwriters who could not stop writing if you handcuffed their hands behind their back, as if possessed.

If you think of someone that is an easily replicable Halloween costume, from Ariana Grande's high ponytail to Michael Jackson's red leather jacket to Madonna's bedazzled boobs, you have an icon. While we praise the aesthetic appearance and reinvention of pop stars, there is also an inherent theory of divine intervention. I remember feeling this way about Lady Gaga in middle school when she wore meat or gigantic bubbles. *How does someone see the world so differently than everyone else?*

Today, I believe that artists are not only valued for their unique and inherent perspective on the world. They are also seen as workhorses who step above and beyond in a hyper-productive society.

Stephen King's memoir, *On Writing*, provides advice from the bestseller mountaintop. King talks about how his son wanted to play the saxophone but couldn't be encouraged to practice. He concluded that since his son rarely wanted to play the saxophone, he should quit. If King's son couldn't find the natural motivation to play, he would never succeed.

"Talent renders the whole idea of rehearsal meaningless; when you find something at which you are talented, you do it (whatever *it* is) until your fingers bleed or your eyes are ready to fall out of your head," King writes. "Even when no one is listening (or reading, or watching), every outing is a bravura performance, because you as the creator are happy. Perhaps even ecstatic."

We have to trust he's got some insight as an inky fingered author with sixty-seven books and 200 short stories from worlds and societies he created from his imagination.

Though writing for the sake of validation is an unsatisfying motivation, King suggests if there is any pain or discomfort around creating, then perhaps you are not meant to create. Perhaps your passion is not your passion at all.

This is an idea that terrifies me every day. It makes me feel that there is something wrong with me that I face any friction in my writing process. I should be gliding if I was meant to do this! As a self-scolding perfectionist who has convinced myself of having no talent, I fear that other people have less creative inertia. It becomes an immeasurable and harsh comparison. Did the greats feel like this? Or am I forcing it? I can never know.

Malcolm Gladwell used the Beatles as an example of his ten-thousand hour chapter of *Outliers*. The Beatles opened at a strip club in Homberg, Germany, for eight hours a day, seven days a week for 1,200 shows. By the time they came to America, their careers exploded into Beatles-mania. Gladwell states the process didn't happen overnight, which would imply luck or fate. It happened over a series of ten thousand hours playing together.

As the ten-thousand-hour rule becomes common knowledge, it is both optimistic and daunting. The resource all of us have is time. Any of us could put 10,000 hours toward something. Again, it puts pressure on every free minute. Instead of sitting on the couch, we could spend the time writing and clocking in expertise one hour at a time.

Since *Outliers'* 2008 publication, this theory of hard work has infiltrated mainstream conversation and influenced contemporary experts. For example, Billie's producing partner and brother, Finneas, has "10,000 hours" scribbled into the doorway to his bedroom where Billie and Finneas produce her music.

People may have natural talent, we tell ourselves, but any of us can work toward being a professional. We can make our own paths! Disciplined effort has become the new benchmark for success, implying that anyone can make their own success.

Dr. Angela Duckworth's 2016 book *Grit: The Power of Passion and Perseverance* reflects on how her father commented on how she and her siblings weren't "geniuses," yet she grew up to be a MacArthur Fellow, colloquially known as the Genius Grant. Duckworth believes that her work ethic, not her natural skill, placed her in this coveted position and unpacks the assumptions and benefits around grit in her book.

Though Duckworth cites that Americans are twice as likely to say they favor effort over talent compared to those from other countries, she points out an unconscious bias toward "prodigy" or "natural talent" in a blind orchestra audition study. The violinist who is described as "a natural" plays, then the violinist described as "gritty" plays. The deciding committee prefers the naturally gifted violinist, though Duckworth reveals it was the same violinist playing both auditions.

She calls this "a hidden preference for those who we think arrived at their place in life because they're naturally talented." We prefer a natural talent, but if we want to be successful ourselves, we need to be gritty. Natural talent could mean nothing if the talented person doesn't turn their talent into a hustle.

Based on these ideas, I started to believe that any inky fingered person from Fiona Apple to Stephen King has a different natural talent: a limitless love of what they do. The Beatles performed long hours in that strip club *because they loved to play.* Billie Eilish and Finneas were homeschooled to pursue whatever path they wanted to in life, *and they chose music as if called to a vocation.*

Prodigies are no longer born. They are made. They don't break one pen in their hand. They break two or three pens a day, amid sleep or daybreak, and they buzz through a masterpiece in two months. Their talent is not their craft but their fearlessness in pursuing it, as if they were born without the fear to put pen to paper.

In holding this idea so close to me, it paralyzes me. I could be a real writer if I just put in the time. If I could be a real writer, I might make a difference in this world. I could be someone to someone else. I could have the calm creative satisfaction Billie has in her interviews.

There's nothing wrong with the ambition or passion to write more. What is painful about this for me is there's also an inherent jab in my perfectionism. I believe that there is something wrong with me that puts me behind. If I was supposed to write, I would just write. Instead, I tell myself, "You'll never get anywhere because you were never meant to get anywhere. You aren't a natural, and you're not gritty. You have nothing to say."

Most days, with this pressure to cut through the noise inside and outside my head, I don't even pick up the pen. If I can't advocate to myself to sit down and write something no one else will see, how can I promote anything I write to an audience?

THINK ABOUT IT

"Nowadays, as a singer, songwriter, you are everything," Ava Baker told me. "You're your own social media marketing, manager, your own tour booker. You do it all. And that used to not be the case. Like all you had to do is focus on making music and touring and fostering more creativity. And now there's so many things to do."

Ava Baker is on the cusp of a move to Los Angeles. Most days, she nannies full-time, comes home, and works on her music for four hours between dinner and bed. In 2020, she designed a website, produced a line of merchandise, and created Instagram updates on her music almost daily. She collaborated on three new singles and wrote a single in response to the Black Lives Matter protests called "Think About It." Most of her free time after work is spent researching market or industry trends, creating social media content, reaching out to independent Spotify playlists, or having writing or recording sessions alone or with other musicians and music producers.

"I have to admit, some days I would say fuck it and not do anything at all, so by no means do I want to falsely represent this grinding musician who lives, breathes, and eats music. But I was grinding," Ava told me. "I think currently, I'm trying to work on deciding how to best use my time and utilize it for maximum efficiency. I don't think I was as intentional. I was tired and hit burnout."

Talking abstractly about work ethic or discipline for someone starting in a creative field is one thing. However, for someone like Ava, there are more expectations of aspiring singer-songwriters. The "work" is not just the creative flow of singing or songwriting. It is the pressure to build and maintain a personal brand for new fans or music industry professionals.

Creating music has become more accessible in the last ten years. Spotify and Apple Music offer global platforms for emerging artists to be discovered. Ava creates TikToks in her bathroom with a microphone and a ring light. Social media, especially TikTok, allows artists to develop a following where they can make themselves discoverable to a fanbase before being discovered by a record label. Most mainstream pop songs now originate on TikTok in the background of trending videos.

For someone like Ava, this can be a struggle—do you put forward the music that you want to write or create, or do you create something that might have more viral momentum? If Ava is discovered by a music label or a music manager, that industry connection can alleviate some of the personal branding Ava has to do. To be discovered, does she have to make her music fit into what is popular in the hopes the right person sees it?

"Good music is going to do well," Ava said. "If we can just focus on making good music, and not focus on what's the cool sound right now, making music and making it from the heart, it's gonna perform well."

It is easy to look to someone like Billie Eilish who has agents, managers, her family, her crew, and her brother who all function to make her celebrity possible. Compared to Ava, she has the freedom to do whatever she wants since she doesn't have to worry about being discovered. It makes it easier to believe that someday, if we reach a certain level of expertise, it is easier to be creative. But does the work ever end for someone, even after they reach the top?

REPUTATION

In the Netflix documentary *Miss Americana*, Taylor Swift takes the audience into her studio sessions where she and her producers compose verses and choruses for her 2019 album *Lover*. In a clip of Taylor receiving a call that her 2017 album *Reputation* received no Grammy nominations, she holds back tears. "You know what? This is fine. I just need to make a better record," she says. When the rep on the phone tells her *Reputation* is a great record, she denies it and says, "No, I'm making a better record."

What the audience sees is a pop star kicked down, spitting the tooth, and bouncing back to continue creating the next Grammy album. (Stars: they're just like us.) What I saw was a perfectionist.

Besides Billie, whose gift seems as natural as sunrise, Taylor Swift is our generation's demonstration of inky fingers.

Over the pandemic, she wrote the Grammy-winning *folklore*, then released *evermore* a few short months afterward, and then remastered her *Fearless* album.

"To put it plainly, we just couldn't stop writing songs. To try and put it more poetically, it feels like we were standing on the edge of the folklorian woods and had a choice: to turn and go back or to travel further into the forest of this music. We chose to wander deeper in," Taylor wrote in her Instagram post announcing the surprise companion album *evermore*.

While many fans note Taylor's inky fingers—how she pulls out a voice memo with a verse and chorus recorded at 4:30 a.m., how she effortlessly creates lyrics on the fly—it helps to note Taylor's perfectionist tendencies as well.

She outlines how she lived for applause, for strangers' affection by the millions. She worries about being a good girl, a someone-everyone-likes girl. She comments on the appearance of her "dead face," her "really slappable face." She confesses to an eating disorder because of media coverage of her body. She ruminates on how female music artists have to reinvent themselves twenty times more than men do (look at John Mayer—has that man even gotten a different haircut since his career started?). A montage of her in various sequins and haircuts and costumes and stage set-ups traces her career since fifteen.

She may have inky fingers, but Taylor doesn't have an easier road to creation than any of us. She reads aloud a journal entry from May 2003 when she practiced songs she wrote but broke down crying: "I want it so bad, but I get so scared of what might happen." Taylor may have gotten to her 10,000 hours from starting to write at a young age or being naturally inclined toward songwriting, but the perfectionism never leaves.

At one point, she looks at the camera and admits that without her songwriting, her entire career disappears. She believes it's the thing that has and continues to set her apart in the music industry. She writes because she's a professional songwriter, but the internal pressure (that voice that says she needs to make "a better record" after any album) might never leave Taylor.

In *Grit*, Duckworth quotes the philosopher Friedrich Nietzsche to explain our goal toward seeing the successful as untouchably brilliant: "Our vanity, our self-love promotes the cult of the genius. For if we think of genius as something magical, we are not obliged to compare ourselves and find ourselves lacking. To call someone divine means here, there is no need to compete."

It is easier for me, in my perfectionism, to consider someone else's greatness to contrast my lack. In a beautiful way, it is wonderfully uniting to think perfectionism connects me to Taylor Swift. We have the same fears in entirely different lives.

If I promote Taylor as a genius, I separate myself from her example. I can imagine that her life is easier or, more daunting still, her level of success would solve any self-doubt I carry. (Shocking, the perfectionist believes she can fix herself by working harder.)

I don't want Taylor Swift's celebrity. What I want is the calm to know I did something right or that my life contributed something. What I want is Billie's sense of self.

HAPPIER THAN EVER

In the *Vanity Fair* interview, the various Billies evolve in video footage against each other. Yes, it's the hair dye changes from ash to blue to green-black, but it's something else, too. There's a peppiness, an evolution of the graveled voice, a settling into a public persona that evolves and grows up in front of the camera.

Her 2018 self, the one whose eyes sit saddest on the camera, said, "I just want to do everything. I want to create what I want to create when I want to create it. It's gonna change, no matter what."

Her 2019 version, no longer blue in hair or attitude, responds to the clip and says, "Same shit. Whatever I want. I'm not going to tell myself to do something different next year. I'm just gonna do what I want next year. That's what I'm doing this year."

In that same interview, *Vanity Fair* asks the 2019 Billie about her songwriting technique. "Honestly, I don't know because I kind of have no idea what to expect. Like, I thought I knew last year. I thought I knew what people would like for my album, and I thought I knew what would be popular, and I was so wrong," Billie says about her debut album. It is the same insecurity Ava faces at the beginning of her career and the same fear that plagues Taylor Swift—what will be the reception when it goes public, and social media measures the song's love, hate, or indifference? Billie can do whatever she wants, but 70 million Instagram followers sit in the studio with her. *What will they like?*

Though perfectionism leaks into each piece of our everyday life, I never considered celebrities experiencing perfectionism. I assumed fame made you free. When you stepped outside the norms, people didn't think twice. They expected that from you. If I stuck a ukulele in my mouth and posted it as a celebrity, they would love it. I'm too scared as a regular person to post a TikTok for anybody, let alone with my mouth full of baby guitar.

In the most recent *Vanity Fair* interview, the 2020 version of Billie is stacked on top of the Billies of the past; she has the same chill and same hair color as her 2019 self. Strikingly vulnerable, she looks more adult. Technically, she is finally an adult in 2020 at eighteen. As the pandemic affected everyone, it impacted music touring with a complete standstill. "The shows are the one thing that I feel like I've ever been good at. I know that sounds stupid, but it's the only thing I've ever done that made me feel like I belonged," Eilish said.

After winning five Grammys, Eilish still feels like she has to prove herself.

Then she says, "For a while now, I've really been having an identity crisis a little." She had a radio show performance in December 2019, and "the entire show, I felt I was pretending to be Billie Eilish." She couldn't see herself as she was. She saw herself as how others saw her, and it happened at other events and award shows. "I just felt like a parody of myself... you forget I'm literally eighteen. It's funny that I'm expected to have found myself and stick with it."

There's a process to fame that echoes that desire to be more, to be what others expect. According to Donna Rockwell, a clinical psychologist studying celebrity mental health, fame moves in stages: loving fame, hating fame, being addicted to fame, accepting fame, *then* adapting to the positive and negative experiences of fame. "The person develops a kind of character-splitting between the 'celebrity self' and the 'authentic self,' as a survival technique in the hyperkinetic and heady atmosphere associated with celebrity life," Rockwell writes. "Some descriptions of fame include feeling like 'an animal in a cage; a toy in a shop window; a Barbie doll; a public facade; a clay figure; or that guy on TV.'"

Billie herself has mentioned how she wanted to go to Trader Joe's without being recognized but couldn't even leave her house when her star was first rising. Now, she appreciates that she is the one who experiences the fame she has, even if it cost the chance to ever run a public errands.

"Maybe people see me as a rule-breaker because they themselves feel like they have to follow rules, and here I am not doing it," Billie told *Vogue*. "That's great, if I can make someone feel more free to do what they actually want to do instead of what they are expected to do. But for me, I never realized that I was expected to do anything. I guess that's what is actually going on—that I never knew there was a thing I had to follow. Nobody told me that shit, so I did what I wanted."

It's that do-you-see-rules-I-don't perspective that makes me wish I could step inside her mind. All I see are rules. What would I be able to see if I could subtract the rules I bury myself with, the "always" and "never" generalizations that follow me day-to-day? What is life without a formula?

The simpler question is if nobody told me what to do, what would I want to do? If I didn't have to put pressure on myself to be inky fingered or a critical success, would I still write? I can be the most disciplined person in the world like Taylor Swift, but would that make me happy if I can't stop thinking about what is next? If I'm always seeking someone to tell me I've made it and reached success?

In her Carpool Karaoke interview, James Corden pulls out a ukulele from the backseat after offering a corny "do you play the ukulele?" lead-in. She strums and sings the first song she ever wrote on a playdate. She was seven. This older

Billie, the one in the car, flicks her fingers over the strings and recalls the childhood lyrics of playing in grass and literally smelling the roses. She sandwiches each lyric between the repetitive statement that this life is a wonderful life.

Maybe making something is that simple. It might not be about labels or success or acclaim. Maybe it's just a playdate.

That's the place where I can pick up my pen and start to work it out.

CHAPTER 4:

THE HAMILTON ETHOS

———

That staccato opening hit. Piano keys pound offstage in an imitation march, then slide into a slight waver. Michelle Obama snaps along to the beat, and Barack smiles. In 2009, at the White House, Lin-Manuel Miranda re-introduces a forgotten founder.

The audience freezes as Miranda explains how this unnamed protagonist worked harder and smarter to be better than everyone else, to grant himself opportunities that no one else would give him.

When Miranda breaks into the chorus to introduce the name of our self-starter—Alexander Hamilton—the audience breaks the trance and laughs.

A few moments earlier, when Miranda first walked onto the stage as an acclaimed writer nominated for Tonys, a Grammy, and a Pulitzer Prize in Drama for *In the Heights*, his hands shook. "I'm thrilled the White House called me tonight," Miranda says. "Because I'm actually working on a concept album about somebody who I think embodies hip hop: Treasury Secretary Alexander Hamilton."

The crowd laughed then, too. They imagined Miranda was joking. A white man in a powdered wig...as the personification of hip-hop? It doesn't compute, even for the creative crowd at the White House's Evening of Poetry, Music, and Spoken Word.

"You laugh! But it's true!" Miranda yells.

Miranda sings through the audience's playful disbelief in his thesis, his voice wobbling as he sings about the people in the wings for Hamilton's approach, unaware how, in seven years from this moment, he would wait in the wings for a Grammy-winning and Tony-winning chorus to introduce him as Hamilton on Broadway.

This wacky pitch became *Hamilton,* the record-breaker. Whatever it touched made bank, a fitting tribute to the Treasury founder. It not only broke Tony records with sixteen nominations, but when Broadway closed due to the pandemic, *Hamilton* had grossed nearly $650 million over 1,916 performances with tickets listed at $375. That's an average revenue of approximately $339,000 per performance. That doesn't include resale tickets, which could reach up to $2,000 a ticket according to a 2016 *Business Insider* article.

To put that in perspective, *Hamilton* in five years made half the revenue of *Phantom of the Opera,* the longest-running Broadway show at thirty-two years. Another comparison? *Wicked,* debuted in 2003, grossed over $1.3 billion. A huge chunk of change. But *Wicked* performed over *12 million shows,* putting their average show revenue at $112.15 compared to *Hamilton*'s $339,000.

What is it about *Hamilton* that resonates? Critics called its Broadway opening "a game-changer" (*Deadline*), "that strange and that spectacular" (*Entertainment Weekly*), "a triumph" and "a game-changing figure in musical history"

(*Hollywood Reporter*). *The New York Times* review is my favorite. It's opening line? "Yes, it really is that good."

What is it about *Hamilton* that captivates a global audience, revolutionized live theater on stage and on screen, and makes me cry? (Maybe two or three times if I'm being honest?)

Perhaps the question I should ask instead is that first lyric of the show: *how*.

**

As Christopher Jackson's George Washington sings "One Last Time" to recreate Hamilton and Washington's writing of Washington's Farewell Address, a phrase flashed across my brain from history class: *American exceptionalism*. One of the founding principles that Washington left behind for the American people after he left office.

"Where is the security for property, for reputation, for life, if the sense of religious obligation desert the oaths which are the instruments of investigation in Courts of Justice?" Washington wrote. To paraphrase, Washington believed morality was the American identity. From the country's birth as a democratic power, Washington instilled the ambition to become the example for other countries, determined to be better. The first American dream rested in moral superiority.

As a country, America's individualistic identity has leaked into its citizens' thoughts. How closely do we, as twenty-first century Americans, still hold onto that revolutionary identity of righteousness? As individuals, how much of that patriotic identity of forging a new path seeped into our history?

With my limited expertise in American history, think of the highlight reel: Revolutionary War, Civil War, pioneer trails, the World Wars, the (passive-aggressive) Cold War.

As the country expanded with immigrants from all over the globe, the definition of the country stayed the same: the land of the free. Free to do what you want. America promised to be perfect, a global lighthouse guiding other countries by the democratic principles they exemplified to the world.

In the twentieth century, Americans have moved away from holding onto their country's identity and fragmented into large demographics within the whole. White consumer culture has turned suburbia into a competition of keeping up with the Joneses. Civil rights protesters and conscientious objectors demonstrate that the government's rules are not always right and should not be blindly followed.

As America ignores the contradictions to its moral identity, it homes in on the individual in the seventies, Anne Helen Petersen writes in *Can't Even*. Coming off a decade of assassinations and documented violence in Vietnam and Birmingham, the seventies' "Me Generation," a term Tom Wolfe labeled the post-hippie generation of spirituality and Scientology, allowed people to ignore national problems to focus on individual improvement.

"The cult of the individual elides all the ways in which the individual's hard work was able to take root and flourish because of federally implemented programs and policies, from the Homestead Act to the G.I. Bill—programs that often excluded people who were not white or male," Petersen writes. "But it's easier—and more heroic—if the story of middle-class ascendancy is all about individual hard work."

In a country where the American dream focuses on hard work—anyone can be anyone if they put in the effort—shifts from a national morality to an individual ambition. If a citizen can do everything right, they can transcend any barrier. Take control of your own destiny through your own actions.

In this America, President Reagan walks into the Oval Office.

**

When Reagan was a child, his aunt took him to have his shoes cobbled, and young Reagan couldn't decide whether he wanted rounded or square toes. The cobbler nodded and said the shoes would be ready in a few days. When Reagan picked up his new shoes, one shoe had a rounded toe, and one shoe had a square toe.

"This will teach you never to let someone else make your decisions for you," the cobbler said.

"I learned right then and there," Reagan said, "if you don't make your own decisions, someone else will."

The Reagan Revolution hinged on power to the individual with his anti-union legislation, trickle-down economics, and stripped welfare programs. Whoever works hard enough will find economic success, no matter the institutional obstacles they might face due to race, gender, or ability. The power of individual decision—each person as the maker of their own fate—influenced his political legacy.

If society seemed unstable coming off the late sixties and seventies, then the idea of an individual's power over their life provided ointment to those who worried their status was at risk. Wider social change isn't needed; people need to change themselves. Why would I be responsible for my neighbor if they cannot be responsible for themselves? When Donald Trump revived Reagan's "Make America Great" slogan for his 2016 campaign, he signaled that greatness, or that moral premise of individual power under Reagan, did not have to die in a post-Obama America.

While Washington's exceptionalism warned of foreign interference, its premise of moral superiority never left. It moved into our homes and workspaces. The American dream is a collective dream, a faint hope tinged with cynicism now that still beckons that we could just work a little harder, be a little better in all aspects of our lives.

In 2019, *Atlantic* writer Derek Thompson wrote that careers have replaced religion's role in our society as Americans have secularized. "A lot of people have essentially turned to work to find the very things that they used to seek from traditional religions," Thompson said. "Transcendence, meaning, community, self-actualization, a totalizing purpose in life. And so I think in many ways, we have essentially made our work our God."

Thompson's "workism" demonstrates that Americans, if leaning on morality for their definition of the exceptional American life, must measure it in their work. Our work has become the beacon for how we define ourselves, not only on LinkedIn, but in our principles. While Washington suggested that we derive our morality from a religious sense of principle, we as a population, have replaced our own morals with the capitalist principles of a good employee—keep working until you feel transcendent satisfaction.

This optimization has leaked into the way I view my own life, especially as a perfectionist. I find myself wanting to itemize my happiness, run down my day and pick out happy moments; weigh the costs against the benefits to say if the day was worth something. How can I improve for tomorrow? How can I be a better writer, employee, girlfriend, daughter, friend? Is there an example of a good life that I can CTRL+C to ensure my life, at its end, was fully maximized, used to its highest potential?

And the cleanest answer, if we allow workism to dictate how we orient our lives, would be...work.

**

Delanie Fischer left during her lunch break for a quick walk, and her mind cleared.

Not cleared as in meditative euphoria. Cleared like a system reboot.

She couldn't think of anything, remember where she had to be, focus on any particular outing. "My body just stopped," Delanie said. While this occurrence for an older woman might signal early symptoms of dementia, Delanie's brain stopped working because of burnout.

To any comedy-minded person from the outside, myself included, Delanie's accomplishments were pretty amazing. Through the lens of workism, which hopes for a purpose-assuring satisfaction in our work, Delanie had found success in the most creative comedy realms. The day she burnt-out, she was actively committed to the following:

- Working full-time on a studio lot
- Performing stand-up several times a week in landmark LA comedy clubs and on television
- Writing and revising her second network screenplay
- Preparing for acting auditions
- Writing packets (a bunch of jokes and sketches) to be considered as a late-night TV staff writer
- Improvising with her troupe
- Launching a side hustle passion project of penis-portrait mugs called Dicks by Delanie
- Hosting the *Self-Helpless* podcast to explore self-help with fellow comedians Taylor Tomlinson and Kelsey Cook

In the neat bullet points of a quasi-resume, the accomplishments couldn't get much cooler. She seemed on the brink of something bigger, as if it was a matter of time (and, of course, continued effort) before one of these things turned into something even BIGGER, more impressive, and more creatively satisfying. She had mild symptoms of burnout, losing track of where she was supposed to be and when, but someday, she hoped, there would be results for the work she was putting in.

"I felt like a machine, you know," Delanie said, "just trying to collect trophies and certificates and awards and accolades and TV credits and all this stuff without actually asking myself, do I like doing any of this? Am I actually enjoying my life? Because I'm so focused on the result of the thing that I'm not even asking myself if I'm enjoying the process of getting there."

She had to change how she was living.

After her burnout factory-reset her thoughts, Delanie made a list of everything she was doing, and she started to cross things out. Some of these things, no matter how awesome or cool they were, no matter how they might open a door in the future, had to go. With her list in front of her, she wanted to do the podcast with her friends, and she wanted to paint phallic mugs. Everything else on the list were activities that distracted her from her long-term goals.

She called her manager and said she no longer wanted to pursue acting and stopped writing packets. She emailed the network that she wouldn't be writing the screenplay. She texted her improv troupe that her next show would be her last. She wrapped a ribbon on her stand-up career with a special called *Love at First Cousin* about first cousin relationships, inspired by her mom's rendezvous with her own British first cousin. Within a year, she quit her corporate studio job to do Dicks by Delanie full-time.

Today, she is still hosting the *Self-Helpless* podcast and runs her own coaching business. It would be easy to look at the success of both of those things to turn this story into an example for others looking to optimize their own lives— Open up your bandwidth! Master your craft! Quit your day job! But Delanie's satisfaction doesn't come from working toward a desired end result. It comes from appreciating the day-to-day life she lives.

"Now I prioritize enjoyment and things I love doing over accolades any day," she says, comparing her previous burnout lifestyle to her life today. "Like I did that, it wasn't for me. It wasn't sustainable. I burned out. I was not happy. And now I will turn down accolades and those types of things and opportunities that somebody else might really enjoy because it just doesn't align with how I want to spend my time."

Though the pandemic has put a spotlight on the work-life balance issue as the physical lines of workspace and home disappeared, there was still that impulse to be productive no matter what. When I hear Delanie's story, I think of how I thought, "*Finally! Now that all my things are cancelled, I will have time to write!*" My life was simplified, yet I was still unsatisfied.

Days slipped through my fingers where I stood anxiously, wondering how I could make productivity *happen* out of a newly fresh palette. During the day, I caught up on buzzy TV shows that satisfied virtual water cooler conversations and exercised during my lunch break. At night, I spent time with my siblings watching movies or completing jigsaw puzzles, a secret puddle of anxiety because my brain couldn't stop bouncing around. *When are you going to write? Are you going to write at midnight when the movie's done? What if you're just wasting this time? What if at the end of pandemic, you have nothing to show for the time?*

Then, on the eve of the 2020 election, I watched *Hamilton* for the first time, and I felt that hope. Hamilton doesn't just have inky fingers (can the man please stop writing for a SECOND—like, chill).

Watching it rocked me. (And again, I wept at least three times.)

Because Lin-Manuel Miranda's "Hamilton" is a perfectionist.

**

Miranda, in his *Hamilcast* interview, brings up Aesop Rock, an American hip-hop artist from the late 1990s. He asks, "Is there a better example of the *Hamilton* ethos than Lucy in 'No Regrets?'"

Aesop Rock's song "No Regrets" follows Lucy through three verses of childhood, adulthood, old-womanhood. She spends her entire life drawing and holds no meaningful relationships. Her neighbors see her as a weird recluse.

With her last breath, she tells her nurse she never had a dream because she lived her life as she wanted to live it. She didn't have to wish someday she would do what she wanted. She just did it. She drew.

That *Hamilton* ethos is acting out the dream instead of waiting for it to land in your lap. Who better to speak to the *Hamilton* ethos than the person who wrote it into being and perhaps lived it himself?

Lin-Manuel Miranda, himself, is Lucy. He is the Alexander Hamilton of Broadway.

There are so many ingredients that defy Broadway tradition: the hip-hop and rap, the BIPOC cast, the nearly three-hour showtime that stretches beyond most people's attention spans and almost doubles an average show's runtime of ninety minutes. Compared to traditional Broadway, there's no way this could've worked.

You laugh, but it's true.

He broke free from precedent and made something unforgettable—like Hamilton himself. It's that rise-to-the-top story of a bastard orphan packaged in the modern version of that Hamilton figure in contemporary culture. He doesn't wait for it. Miranda moves forward with his idea despite the established norms of Broadway musicals.

It took Miranda seven years. Hard years of self-doubt and revising and performing the female falsettos on his demos to recreate the idea bouncing around in his head. He wrote "Wait For It" on the subway to a friend's birthday party. When he arrived at the party, he wished his friend a happy birthday and got back on the subway to finish the song. After reading Ron Chernow's Hamilton biography on vacation, Miranda immediately Googled "Hamilton musical" because the idea was so clear to him, he couldn't believe no one else had done it. He saw something no one else did and grew it, just like the Founding Fathers. He turned his job and passion into a world-shaking $600 million event.

"One of the hallmarks of genius is an ability to spot connections between seemingly disparate things and then go on to create something that reveals the world in a new light," *Vogue* wrote about Miranda. Even in the face of a 2009 White House crowd laughing at his idea, Miranda held close to his idea and pushed to make it happen.

"Lin is so unapologetically himself," Daveed Diggs, Grammy-winning Jefferson of the original *Hamilton* cast said to *Vogue*, "and that's undefeatable."

It is easy to fall into and consume the narrative—of Miranda's recreated Hamilton and Miranda's own success—that work is the answer. That is the American dream, then, now, forever. Work hard and make never-before-seen changes. Disrupt everything from democracy to Broadway. We all want to believe that our work will someday lead to satisfaction, or that our own names will land somewhere in print or lights.

We want to believe a piece of us will be left behind because we orient our lives around our individual success.

We ignore the tragedy of the time Hamilton lost with his family. The summer in the Hamptons. The time with his son before he died. Nothing is enough. They left Eliza in the dust with nothing but her love to fuel her to her old age. The Hamilton character's downfall is his moral superiority, and this diligence to principle cost him his and his son's lives.

Eliza's life, though pained with the loss of her husband and son, seems the most fruitful. She loves. She works within the community, not for a historical legacy (as she shows in "Burn" that she's not preoccupied with her piece in his narrative centuries later), but out of love for her husband. She founds an orphanage and works in his honor, while he worked for the abstract value of democracy and himself.

Her legacy wasn't about optimizing the best life or country. She was an otherwise forgotten wife, alongside a previously forgotten man, who filled her life by giving to the people she loved. In the fictionalized birthplace of the individual and democracy, Eliza loved the man who, despite all his accomplishments, claimed he would never be satisfied.

PART 2

"It is just not that deep."

—MY PARENTS

CHAPTER 5:

THE RAMSAY ROAST

———

One adolescent Sunday rings in my head as all adolescent Sundays. From the sectional, my mom watches Bravo and folds hand-me-down dresses and grease-shadowed tee shirts. My dad next to her folds clothes and places them in a cracked laundry basket. My siblings and I gaze in bent-neck hypnosis at the TV. It's one glimpse into one day, but it reinforces my belief that I grew up on a diet of *Top Chef* marathons.

There's the echo of the New York *Top Chef* season on Bravo in the background: quirky and chipper Carla, Fabio as one-half of "the Europeans," and the Leah and Josiah flirtation. In one episode, Fabio, the charismatic Italian, digs at another contestant for her repetitive seafood: "It's *Top Chef*, not 'Top Scallops!'" We all laugh, the phrase tattooed in the family lexicon, though we never ate seafood. Feeding fish or scallops to six kids under ten could be expensive *and* thrown out, a double risk. The fanciest food haunting my childhood is a Pillsbury French loaf my mom drowned in marinara and shredded mozzarella. Pizza bread was the biggest culinary adventure in our house.

On my breaks from college or Manhattan, I return home to my parents, siblings, and pups and curl up to watch *The Great British Baking Show, Nailed It!* or *Chopped.* We wager that the contestant crying about missing their three-month-old newborn or about their deceased mom at the top of the show will win by the end. Or be eliminated. When I return to my apartment, my roommates and I laugh at the college contestants on *Chopped.* We heckle at the kids who speak haughtily about growing up in New York. Then I go to Luke's apartment and watch *Hell's Kitchen*'s early seasons and involuntarily laugh as Gordon Ramsay calls the women stupid cows.

As much as I cringe watching him insult his contestant's intelligence, Ramsay ironically is a soothing watch. He serves the scalding heckles I would only feel comfortable delivering to a TV screen.

Ramsay paved his international reputation as the man who spits out food, smashes plates, and drops the f-bomb at everyone but the child contestants on *MasterChef Junior* (I assume…I hope). His ten-year stint at *Hell's Kitchen* has germinated nineteen other executively produced shows according to Ramsay's IMDb, seven of which broadcast the "Ramsay" name in the title and three of which (*Kitchen Nightmares, MasterChef USA,* and *MasterChef Junior*) have grown into their own household names.

As linear TV fails to grip younger generations, Ramsay has expanded his personality to social media where he perpetuates his iconic "fuck off" personality into a household— or rather, phone-hold—name for another generation. Case in point? Ramsay's daughter Tilly posts TikToks with Gordon that garner anywhere from 30 million to 100 million views.

A viral meme (which I sourced from the YouTube page "Random Memes") claimed to have footage from the unreleased British version of the Pixar movie, *Ratatouille*. It cuts to the cartoon restaurant where Remy, the rodent protagonist, has a new voiceover. Instead of Patton Oswalt's kid-friendly voice, it's Ramsay's raspy voice yelling insults: "You serve me shit like that, take off your jacket, and FUCK OFF;" "You're fucking pathetic;" "SAUCE!"

Chef contestants, cartoon rats, and amateurs are eligible for Ramsay's verbal lashings. He's notorious for ripping people apart on Twitter for their terrible meal pictures. Again, he seems to spare kids, which is redeeming. My friend and I used to watch video compilations of someone reading Ramsay's Tweets and would die laughing as each Twitter user sent their hopeful picture of a meal they cooked, looking for validation. The tone always seemed a little too hopeful: "What do you think, chef?"

Then Ramsay eviscerated them to his thousands of followers.

"You've got a great future in my industry...as a customer," Ramsay Tweeted as a response to a plate with a culinary-enough sauce swoosh. "Idiot sandwich" comes with an implied trademark symbol from him.

In the pilot episode of *Hell's Kitchen,* Ramsay justifies his brutality: "I've always extracted the best out of individuals because I push them to the absolute max. That's how you get perfection."

What a monster.

Or is he?

The five-time Emmy-nominated *Hell's Kitchen* has twenty seasons from 2005 to 2021. Luke and I watched it at his apartment and in his childhood home with his mom. As we all watched, there's something great about watching other people be...terrible. Terrible at what they want to be good at. Terrible to each other. And there's something about the directness of someone telling someone else, to their face, that they're terrible. That aggression, whether it is bitter angst in the confessional interviews or Ramsay saying someone is more "dog-faced than I am" (this in reference to an impatient customer), drives the cooking competition.

In 2014, Sonali Kohli wrote in *The Atlantic* that the Food Network had pivoted from cooking shows a la *Emeril* and shifted toward the *Iron Chef* competition model that premiered on the network in 2000: "Over the past fifteen years, The Food Network has made big profits by turning the kitchen into an ever-more-stressful place." She tracks how the models shifted toward high-pressure show formats like *Chopped, Beat Bobby Flay,* and *Cutthroat Kitchen* (do we just have to protect *The Great British Bake-Off* with our lives?). By 2014, the Food Network claimed that their move toward competitions taught the audiences more because they learned how to critique food in their lives without tasting it. "Viewers learn to say with authority that a dish 'is lacking in texture' or 'needs a deeper flavor profile,'" Kohli notes. "In essence: less cooking, more judging."

Ramsay's television personality paralleled the cooking show's growth into hyper-competition. A Google search for cooking shows returns pages of listicles ranking the best reality shows to watch, a competition for the best competition show. Alongside the competitive edge in cooking shows, Ramsay's *Hell's Kitchen* success, and the magnified anger that viewers opted into over and over like Pavlovian rats, grew up alongside Twitter's start in 2006. Both Ramsay's and Twitter's platforms endured a pubescent escalation during the newest era of global judgment, where nameless users anywhere in the world could run down your throat and try to make you eat your words.

**

My brother, Collin, on Biden's inauguration sent a since-deleted tweet to our family group chat that read, "It feels like America just tossed the ring into Mordor, restored the heart of Te Fiti, destroyed Voldemort's last horcrux, and took the infinity stones back from Thanos all at the same time." Underneath the screenshot was a stranger's response: a picture of an animated man ripping the skin off his face. Collin told us that the user had deleted the tweet because he had been trolled so hard and deemed the user "had earned the ridicule." Collin texted us, and I quote, "Actions have consequences and if you make a tweet that terrible and send it out into the world, you are opening the door for people to flame your ass."

The account is now private—no retweets ever again from our Marvel and *Moana* fan.

We live in a time where we want to be recklessly mean. It's much easier to troll, to assume divisions. It's also much easier for me to yell at the TV screen when someone misses a lay-up clue on *Wheel of Fortune* (though, in their defense, those writers have been amping up the difficulty there...so it makes sense if not everyone gets every clue right even from the couch...just saying). If someone somewhere is not going to do something perfectly, whatever our personal yet assumed universal definition of perfection is, then we can flame their ass.

As discussed in the first chapter, perfectionism comes in three layers. It affects how we view ourselves, society, and others. In others-oriented perfectionism, perfectionists have the tendency to subconsciously hold everyone else in their lives to the impossible standards they hold for themselves. Dr. Samantha Rodman discusses one of her patients, "Anna." As a perfectionist, Anna woke up at 4:45 a.m., went to the gym, came back by 7 a.m. to make sure her kids got to school, and arrived after 9 a.m. to work daily. Her late arrivals caused friction with her boss. When she tells this to her husband, her husband suggests she give up going to the gym in the mornings or cleaning the house for forty-five minutes after the kids leave.

Because Anna is a perfectionist, she feels defensive about her choices being questioned. She doesn't want to accommodate her schedule or compromise on the routine she has already perfected. Perfectionist all-or-nothing thinking will have Anna believe that she needs to complete her routine as is or else she will fall short every morning, which puts a lot of pressure on herself. She feels stressed. She needs to keep her routine intact.

She tells herself she can't change a thing, so instead, Anna lashes out at her husband. If her standards are this high for her mornings, she will also expect him to structure his morning routine like hers. He doesn't, and therefore, this might be his fault.

"Anna tells her husband it is his fault she is late every day. If he cleaned the house with her every evening, then she wouldn't have to clean so much in the morning. She says he may be fine with getting fat and lazy in his middle age, but physical fitness is important to her. There is no way around going to the gym," Dr. Rodman retells. (The fat and lazy thing also isn't something you can apologize away post-fight, am I right? That's coming up in therapy.)

In this perfectionist culture, we distort our self-image to use negativity as motivation, and we hold these high standards to other people. If we want to honk our horn and yell out our window when driving, then so be it because that idiot didn't turn on their blinker on a left turn! Why not throw a fit because McDonald's stops selling sausage biscuits in the afternoon? And my husband could never understand that I care about my body because he's fat and lazy! Yet, for all this goal prescription, when people meet our perfection standards, they become competition. Why can't everyone else be less accomplished and intelligent and toned, please? (This all being thought while eating a loveless McDouble after 11 a.m. and dreaming of the sausage biscuit.)

When I watch reality TV from the safety of my couch, it's easy for me to verbally annihilate contestants for their poorly textured paella or their nasal voice on the reality show that proves they're much more qualified than I am, watching them cook while I can't get off my couch to microwave rice. There's a joy in watching someone else fail while I don't attempt anything.

Schadenfreude, German for "pain joy," is that *America's Funniest Home Videos* brand of humor that comes from others making mistakes. According to Ph.D. candidate Shensheng Wang, some studies have found this reaction to laugh at others who have wronged them in study subjects as young as four years old, two years old, even nine months old. The four-year-olds laughed harder if their peer—if you can call a four-year-old a peer—had busted up someone's toys beforehand. There is something karmic and safe in watching others fail. By villainizing reality TV chefs or making them out to be—in Ramsay's words—"idiots," it's easier to root for them to fail, as if they have earned failure. And this sells.

I love to villainize the unfortunate or less skilled contestants (an unforeseen yet tragically preventable kitchen equipment malfunction is a true thrill), but I have adopted its formula. When you watch enough of these shows, you learn when to cheer or boo. The show itself is a recipe of peaks and valleys, of failures and triumphs.

To paraphrase that *Ratatouille* critic, it is a *delight*.

While *Top Chef* contestants risk time away from their newborns and their immense debt and their jobs and their restaurants, I yell at the TV like I already have the answers. "Oh no, are those baby pictures of Harold from his childhood? He's either winning or going home tonight, I'm calling it. After that warm gazpacho? He's lucky to be here. His head hasn't been in the game since the gazpacho," I say, then scratch at my thighs as a preventative measure against bedsores.

Reality TV echoes two ends of perfectionist extremes in its contestants that beat themselves up (sometimes physically with the ridiculous *Cutthroat Kitchen* stunts) to be the best, and the risk-averse audience hecklers. Brian Swider et al. in the *Harvard Business Review* dissect perfectionism into two branches, excellence-seeking perfectionism and failure-avoiding perfectionism. One group actively evaluates themselves and others against their high standards, and the other uses self-restriction as a protective measure from failure. (This should sound familiar based on the perfectionist pendulum in Chapter 2.)

Maybe this hard shell we form—the heckling and trolling, the jabs at the reality show contestants and scoffs at cheesy tweets—is the exoskeleton of the perfectionist. They tell themselves they will never meet their own standards, so they resent other people's success. We imagine that there's only enough room for one person to be good, and that person is named in the grand finale. I don't even want to be a chef, but someone else's success threatens my success in some sense—so why not make fun of the fact that Harold accidentally left the fridge door open overnight? Warm gazpacho and room-temp raw chicken? A recipe to pack your knives and go.

**

Mellini Kantayya in her book *Actor. Writer. Whatever.: essays on my rise to the top of the bottom of the entertainment industry* opens her book,

Overnight success stories abound, yet at any given time, ninety-seven percent of the 120,000 members of the Screen Actors Guild are unemployed. Ninety-five percent of Sundance films don't get distribution. Novels, poems, and plays sit in dusty desk drawers everywhere. This is the plight of the rank-and-file Actor, Writer, Whatever. These are my people. Fuck those overnight success freaks.

Throughout the essays, she writes from this tortured and bitterly funny perspective of someone who is trying but has accepted that they may have reached the top of their success, even though it's far from fame and acclaim. It's soothing to read if you categorize yourself under her definition of "my people." Or if you like seeing people confess to being terrible at something, which…I also do? (Yikes!)

When I first read this book, I was shocked to find the anxieties I had felt about my own non-success written on a page. I had been wondering if I would ever find success in today's riptide of aspiring writers. I watched an independent short film and thought that any other actor could fill the spots of a Black man, a brunette white woman, a racist old white man—as if actors and creatives could be replicated and mass produced on a conveyor belt. I also held this perspective that no one was special—that the overwhelming supply of creative people washed everyone into mediocrity. Someone once told me to audition for a diversity scholarship at the comedy theater Upright Citizens Brigade, and I replied, as a brunette white girl in Warby Parkers, "I'm just like everyone else." (To be fair, there were a lot of white Warby women at UCB wanting to be Liz Lemon—which was also me.)

It seemed the more I stepped into entertainment, through improv classes or internships, everyone wanted the same general thing: creative passion, steady paycheck. Writing, comedy, video production, storytelling—but make it corporately stable. *If all these people are going for it, too,* I thought, *why would I ever stand out? What if I had the best ideas but got caught in the bottleneck of surplus creatives?*

Actor. Writer. Whatever. was the first time I heard that pessimism rebounded from someone else. Kantayya had a recurring stint on a soap opera and was the first South Asian woman to do so, but she is embarrassed that her resume doesn't show roles from more prestigious shows. She cries in a Trader Joe's wondering if all of this time invested will never result in recognition—or a paycheck more than her husband's teaching salary. She hates affirmations but holds some belief that she might be different from all the other dreamers. I inhaled Kantayya's book like nicotine, holding it in my lungs.

In one of her later chapters, in the same humorous skepticism, Kantayya outlines the scarcity mentality, the belief that everything—resources, success, happiness—has limits in distribution. "Perhaps the theory bears out with intangibles like friendship, love, or recognition. But in regard to tangible assets like money, jobs, or natural resources, even the philosophy's most ardent subscribers would struggle to hold their position in a debate with an economist, a geophysicist, or an Actor, Writer, Whatever." These people know how to measure scarcity in opportunities. Only the top people with the best everything, be it connections or talent or luck, would be selected to live out my dream.

Brené Brown on Oprah's *SuperSoul Conversations* podcast also defines America as a scarcity culture, especially post-9/11. "I started my research six months after 9/11," Brown said. "We are afraid. I would say the last twelve years have been marked by deep fear in our culture. It's like a collective post traumatic response." Once America's sense of security shattered in the wake of the 9/11 attacks, everyone harbored fear for a sense of control and protection. We assume everything is scarce, that it can be taken, that nothing is ever as full as it could've hypothetically been.

"There's a thin film of terror wrapped around us. So, it's I'm not safe enough, I'm not secure enough. It's I'm not liked enough, I'm not promoted enough, I'm not loved enough. I don't have enough," Brown said.

This scarcity mentality feeds into perfectionism by believing something has to be extraordinary to create joy. Brown quotes herself in *I Thought It Was Just Me,* saying, "We seem to measure the value of people's contributions (and sometimes their entire lives) by their level of public recognition. In other words, worth is measured by fame and fortune. Our culture is quick to dismiss quiet, ordinary, hardworking men and women. In many instances, we equate *ordinary* with *boring,* or even more dangerous, *ordinary* has become synonymous with *meaningless*." We all want to find some level of acclaim not only to hear from a wider public that we are liked or approved but also to save ourselves from a seemingly "meaningless" life. In this thought, there's an implication that only some people, the people with the most success, live a meaningful life.

It's exhausting to live in that failure-adverse mentality in a rolling loop of self-criticism. There's something guiding everything I do every day, a slight nag that tells me if I don't, everything could fail. If I don't write or exercise or read or journal, my dream outruns me. Someone else takes the lead.

Perfectionism drives us to protect ourselves from judgment, so we propel judgment at the nearest character with an odd quirk or mildly competitive success.

It's harder to take off the shell and get off the couch and throw ourselves in the competition.

What if someone flames our ass?

**

Ramsay is a self-proclaimed perfectionist, raised in French kitchens where raviolis and tempers flew. "There were some mornings that I woke up with ravioli tucked in my ear and pig's trotter in my shoe," he told Emily Thomas in the podcast *Food Chain*. While working in one of the greatest restaurants in France, he spent his free time at a café observing their kitchen. The café staff thought he was a part-time culinary student because he spent so much of his free time there; they didn't realize he also had a full-time job.

"That was how you learned," Ramsay said.

When I think of Ramsay, I think of this interview with Emily Thomas. Thomas asks him for the five best meals in his life, and he speaks about them with an appreciation for the other chefs who formed him—even the chef who threw raviolis. He spoke of the craft, the meals' simplicity, with a clean admiration, from an expensive rum baba in Southern France ordered on an early, expensive date with his now-wife or the baked egg and cheese soufflé he snuck off unfinished plates after late-night service in his first French restaurant.

His first favorite meal is his mother's mac and cheese. "She'd slice the onions, chop up some smoked bacon, sweat them down, then she'd throw the macaroni in, and she'd throw this incredible cheese sauce over it and literally let it fester, boil, bubble," Ramsay said. His family, with an alcoholic father and an overworked mother, didn't eat decadent meals. Ramsay and his three siblings ate their dinner without thinking about seasoning or texture. They were hungry.

Despite all the potential negativity in his childhood, Ramsay says for his career there was "no better start than watching Mom's face pull it out of the oven, and the tray was all quirky. It was all bent and warped and chipped and dented."

He may demand perfection, and from a scarcity perspective, he may occupy the only mean-chef-with-lots-of-restaurants-and-TV-shows spot available in our cultural index. Some knockoff Gordon Ramsay making his way up the ladder is probably pissed. Though he is an international celebrity, Ramsay seems, at least on the outside, like he could care less about anyone but his mom, his wife, and his kids. He loves what he does, but he holds onto his memories and his people as the core of what he does.

He can be a troll, but he doesn't care who trolls him. His daughter cracks an egg yolk on his head for a TikTok video, and he keeps his cool. And *laughs.* At his own schadenfreude!

The man who trolls people's eggs on Twitter doesn't even flinch when his daughter scrambles yolk in his hair! My perfectionism can remind me that I need to read or exercise because someone else might be getting ahead, sure. I could yell at everyone else in my life for not living up to my standards—and I have. If I stop worrying that I'm the one people will troll or laugh at, then maybe that's wonderful. Maybe that means I don't care what other people dish out to me.

As I write this chapter, I've turned on *Chopped* to watch with my roommate. It's a college episode. The kids are chipper, naïve, and peddling for culinary school money. Their baskets contain roast chicken and tomato soup cans, and the confessional interviews flare up with phrases around Greek life, cafeteria food, and "passion."

"When I talk about it with my fraternity brothers, they don't get that it's not finance or engineering. It's hard for them to wrap their head around the passion and what I want to do moving forward," one of the contestants tells the judges about his young culinary career path.

"That's so mean," my roommate says. I nod.

Then the contestants go into the back room to a makeshift beer pong table while the judges deliberate. My roommate gives me the side-eye again, like "these guys are goobers." I bite my tongue before the judges announce the frat boy will not be chopped after all.

CHAPTER 6:

THE PERFECT PAIRING

CHICKEN PARM

Cooking chicken parm from scratch made me question my principles.

Luke and I planned a getaway at the end of the summer—a week working from home in a Berkshires cabin, post-Labor Day, surrounded by foliage and orchards and a new season—I found myself Googling "fall recipes." I never really cooked. Then all of a sudden, I was planning out the perfect meal plan.

I sent an email with the subject line "berkshires rough meal plan." (It wasn't rough. It was thoroughly thought out.) No salutation, no anything—straight to business:

monday: frozen pizza and red wine. or a light charcuterie board if we're feeling bougie!

tuesday: chicken parm — prep the homemade sauce monday night

wednesday: a nice grilled cheese (with optional bacon &
tomato) w/ tomato soup

thursday: options could be skillet meat & cheese pasta/garlic
sriacha pork stir fry/chicken bacon ranch bake up/french dip
(warning to Luke: there may be vegetables)

potential dessert: cheesy apple crumb bars or apple crisp
with apples from a local orchard

I had lost my damn mind.

The matronly cabin smelled like a dusty attic and had
framed embroidery, cat magnets, and pillows printed with
tree-bark textures. Luke fielded calls from before I woke up to
after I spent all-day reading in various couches. A relaxation
that I had imagined for Luke and me to share became mine
alone as he spent hours in conversations flooded with such
technical jargon that it buzzed through both my ears like a
foreign language. We ended up ordering pizza twice in our
first three nights.

By Wednesday—chicken parm night—we invited our best
friends, Rachel and Matt, to stay with us. They had packed
the car by the time I started simmering the sauce of diced
tomatoes and onion chunks. They navigated the highway as I
butterflied the chicken breasts and punched them through a
Ziploc bag. Luke, headset on, answered work call after work
call and stopped to ask if I could hold on the loud chick-
en-punches shaking the walls until he could mute his microphone. I stopped and started the recipe video for hours and
fluttered around the kitchen. Part of me felt excited about
learning how to do this by scratch; part of me imagined that
we were older than we were, in another generation of dinner

parties, and I was the wife trapped in a kitchen in an apron and petticoat because we invited company.

Rachel and Matt were an hour away, and I split my focus between my recipe, technique, and simmering resentment of Luke's business calls when I remembered Rachel was vegetarian.

I yelled at Luke that he had to order (another) pizza, because I had slathered my hands in temperamental tomato sauce and egg wash. I overheard him on the phone with Rachel and Matt say, "We were making chicken parm and just realized Rachel can't eat that. Is there something else she can eat? Oh, she brought other things. I mean, we can order a pizza." I almost launched his phone into the tomato sauce. *Don't make it sound like I messed up! I thought we were teammates in this!*

The chicken finally came out of the oven about an hour after Rachel and Matt arrived.

Everyone was nice about it.

"Wow, Chlo, this looks amazing," Luke said. He sent a picture to his family group chat.

"I just hope it isn't raw and ends up poisoning us," I said.

Rachel, who brought an apple French toast casserole for breakfast with pre-measured cinnamon and butter in sealed bags and dressing containers, looked at me. "You don't have to beat your stuff up like that," she said.

It wasn't me that I wanted to beat up. I do enough of that, trust me. But Luke was on the chopping block. Mr. Works-So-Hard-He-Can't-Help-Make-Dinner-But-The-Freaking-WOMAN-Can-Do-It-All! Were we on a farm in the Middle Ages? Or in the 1950s?

That spring, I had read an article in *Harper's Bazaar* by Gemma Hartley. She discussed how she wept on Mother's Day while her husband cleaned the bathrooms as her present. Her husband had waited on booking a cleaner, then called one service, deemed them too expensive, and decided—on Mother's Day—that cleaning the bathrooms himself would get the job done. While he cleaned the bathrooms, she watched their kids and picked up the clothes and wrapping paper he left on the ground.

"The gift, for me, was not so much in the cleaning itself but the fact that for once I would not be in charge of the household office work. I would not have to make the calls, get multiple quotes, research and vet each service, arrange payment and schedule the appointment," Hartley writes.

When her husband gets fussy that she doesn't acknowledge how well he cleaned the bathrooms, she has to gently soothe his ego and explain emotional labor. "I was the manager of the household, and being manager was a lot of thankless work. Delegating work to other people, i.e., telling him to do something he should instinctively know to do, is exhausting," Hartley writes. "He restated that all I ever needed to do was ask him for help, but therein lies the problem. I don't want to micromanage housework. I want a partner with equal initiative." She tiptoes around his frustration at her frustration. She can ask him to do something, but he gets annoyed that she has to remind him to do it as if she's pointing out his ineptitude as a partner. This is, by Hartley's definition, a good husband who is a feminist ally and takes on habitual chores like bedtime, dishwashing, and dinners.

Though this article was written in 2017, this invisible line of emotional labor, the burdens placed on the woman in a heterosexual relationship, have dug deeper during the pandemic than 2019's underwire bra straps. (It also human-izes Anna's frustration over a morning routine from the pre-vious chapter.) Four times as many women as men left the workforce in September 2020 as most children returned to school in a virtual or hybrid model. For reference, 865,000 women left the workforce compared to 216,000 men accord-ing to the Center for American Progress. As the childcare industry received little funding from the CARES Act, child-care businesses couldn't reinvent their spaces to be COVID-friendly, and more working mothers had to step back from their jobs to raise their children.

In a separate statistic, between February and October 2020, 2.2 million women lost their jobs, partially because the sectors laying off employees, like healthcare, hospital-ity, retail, and local and state governments, employ a largely female workforce. A year that started with more women in the workforce than men has resulted in the largest flip that has placed women back in 1988 with female employment below fifty-seven percent, disproportionately impacting the employment of Black women and women of color.

As women have to balance between taking care of their aging parents and guiding their children through Zoom school, "the uncomfortable truth is that in their homes, women are still fitting into stereotypical roles of doing the bulk of cooking, cleaning and parenting. It's another form of systemic inequality within a 21st century home that the pandemic is laying bare," according to NPR's Pallavi Gogoi.

Before I went to bed on chicken parm night, I glimpsed at the sink full of pots and pans, bowls and utensils, all sticky and teetering. While Luke played with his cat, who loved the cat-lovers attic vibe, I scrubbed dishes. "You don't have to do that," he said.

"If I don't do it, no one else is going to!" I yell-whispered in that voice of fighting with company over. I didn't mean Rachel and Quinn. I meant Luke. He looked surprised, and the surprise made me angry.

I don't remember how the night ended, with Luke or me or no one finishing the dishes, but I remember feeling scared. Luke is a good one, my best and favorite person. What if we were doomed to fall into these disproportionate domestic and emotional labor divides? What if I end up crying on Mother's Day, drowning in abstract chores while he stands there surprised and confused because I'm upset at labor he has been conditioned to see as invisible?

STARCH WATER

I stayed in a relationship for two years because he promised to be a stay-at-home dad.

In college, I acted as if I had bread to win and couldn't be bothered with any meal more thought-intensive than fried eggs. We cooked on our dates as if running a test trial. "We cooked" meant that he cooked, I watched, and he voiced his technique to teach me. His optimism in teaching me how to cook held a sweetness, a desire to take care, but something else twitched underneath it. He didn't trust me to cut onions (and that was smart, because I didn't and don't know how to cut onions), so he sent me out of the kitchen to grab red wine from Sheetz.

My three years living on campus granted me dining hall privileges, and I don't think I would've eaten if I had to make myself food. I moved through the made-to-order sandwich line hundreds of times, ordering the same maybe-healthy turkey wrap over and over. It was safe and mindless, an assembly line decision. Why cook? Why take the time from myself when I could watch someone else prepare the most time-efficient meal?

For women driven by efficiency in their chase for perfection, Jia Tolentino writes there is always betterment and optimization: "It's very easy, under conditions of artificial but continually escalating obligation, to find yourself organizing your life around practices you find ridiculous and possibly indefensible. Women have known this intimately for a long time." Women turn to barre classes or Sweetgreen salads as they strive for an ideal body. Exercise and salads become the currency toward placating a feminine sense of being "right" or "enough."

Though I considered my butter pasta and grilled cheese as rebellious to our wellness culture (and within my grad-school budget), I had absorbed this same idea with an opposite response. I wanted to pursue an efficient lifestyle that allowed me to move toward optimized life results.

I had started to trust this boyfriend early in the relationship. On one of our first mornings together, I woke up on his couch, hungover and wet. "Did you pee?" he whispered to me. I refused to believe that. "No," I said without thinking about it. I tried to go back to sleep with a theory that I had simply poured a water bottle all over my lap in the middle of the night because I was thirsty. (You know, that classic pour-water-all-over-my-lap thing people do during deep sleep...) He nudged me back awake and proceeded to wash the cushion covers in the laundry room. I watched him do it; neither of us said a word. By the time his roommates woke up at 8 a.m. for a soccer game, they asked where the couch cushions went.

"I was an idiot last night and poured water all over myself," he said. I stared at the floor, fully aware of how thin our excuses were to each other and his roommates. When I left, my eyeballs wanted to fall out of my head from shame and confusion, but my chest relaxed. I found comfort in knowing, in this early stage of our relationship, that this guy would take the reputational hit for me. He did the dirty work, the washing and moving, while shame slowly paralyzed me. Over our two years together, I dissolved into whatever he thought the perfect sorority girlfriend was to keep him. I was friends with his friends, listened to him complain about professors, absorbed his memories of his family and high school friends through stories he told. We measured our seasons together in Greek life formals. We drank too much until our thoughts slurred or bodies went limp. I shielded him from the student-quality late-night show I co-hosted on YouTube and all my short stories. His glimpse into my ambition was the hours I spent away from him at a studio or the library, and the abstract promise that I refused to be the stay-at-home mom. He seemed excited to be a stay-at-home dad.

Our relationship frayed. We drank hard liquor and fought. Our junior year, I wanted to go to *Citizen Kane* in the downtown theater on Valentine's Day. He said he didn't want to, just because. I held onto this for eight months until we broke up. He tried to teach me how to cook marinated chicken in my apartment when my friends left for the bar. I told myself that I had to hold on. In the shower, I imagined that we would end up married and divorced (every girl's fantasy) because something just couldn't work. This disconnect came from the pressure I put on myself to be everything for him, though I also told myself that I needed him to do everything for me. If I left our relationship, who else would ever want to date me? Who else would volunteer to take on the domestic role of stay-at-home parent so I could do whatever acclaim I felt entitled to?

A perfectionist loves nothing more than a formula. Our thinking oscillates between black and white, right and wrong, winner and loser. All I wanted was to take society's traditional gender roles and reverse them. There was no middle ground. I would wear the pants, but not iron them.

Leslie C. Bell wrote in *The Atlantic* about twenty-something women neglecting relationships for self-development: "Many express the same sentiment again and again: 'Why do I, a young and highly educated woman in the 21st century, value relationships with men so highly?' To do so feels like a betrayal of themselves, of their education, and of their achievements." If I became someone's wife, I worried I would have to give up all my diplomas and certificates to appease the role. I believed if I started cooking for my boyfriend, instead of making him cook for me, I would never hand off meal prepping again.

CHICKEN & CAKE

With an Instagram bio that reads "Elevating the everyday," Martha Stewart has turned domesticity into a mainstream art. Around 4 a.m. she feeds the chickens, changes the cat litter, and exercises in her home gym. As she said during a *Good Morning America* interview in 2009 while lifting weights, "Why get sick? Getting sick is a waste of time."

With over sixty books and magazines, syndicated TV shows with Donald Trump and Snoop Dogg, an everyday luxury line at Macy's, a residential community designed and built by her in North Carolina, and an initial public offering that made her the first self-made female billionaire in the United States, Martha conjures a suspension of belief. Women can be stay-at-home forces *and* billionaires if they work hard enough.

"I can almost bend steel with my mind. I can bend any-thing if I try hard enough," Martha told Oprah in *O Magazine* in 2000. "I can make myself do almost anything. But you can get too strong like that, so you have to be careful. You have to temper your strength." (This was before the Feds charged her with obstruction of justice, conspiracy, and securities fraud in 2003.)

She is also one of the most prominent self-proclaimed perfectionists out there. In this interview with Oprah, she confessed she woke up at 4 a.m. to write two columns, exercise, worked with her assistant, and completed another interview, all before seeing Oprah at noon. Though she normally would, Martha withheld making a cake for Oprah's arrival "because you and I don't need a cake!" (What a flex.)

"So, I did a lot of work today already, and it's important to me to be rewarded for that work. If I work that hard, I'd better have results," Martha said.

From her Instagram to her lifestyle, it seems idyllic: an estate in upstate New York, surrounded by chickens and flowers she harvests herself. Part of me wishes that I was a good baker; that I could make cakes in anticipation of my friends coming over. (Seriously, what a life that Martha Stewart *didn't* roll out a cake for Oprah to show how close they are.)

This Martha Stewart lifestyle makes it seem like housework isn't work but beauty. It is a joy to arrange flowers or feed chickens. It is a joy to write cookbooks for a living. Martha lists her daily routine so plainly that a dawn wake-up seems a natural, wholesome component of living in the country. None of it seems like work. (The inky fingers of household chores). When I imagine it, I imagine Martha's clean kitchen with a cake on the white granite counter and no dishes in the sterling sink. There is something beautiful, even desirable, about it for me, but I never translate this beautiful scene to my teeny apartment.

Martha learned about the domestic arts watching her mother. As the second of six kids, she helped her family with chores and balanced her strong academic record. She was the first child to complete a comprehension test at her local library that granted her access to the adult library, where she tore through autobiographies in third grade.

"I was the girl next door," Stewart said. "I was the girl that all parents held up as the example to their daughters. 'Why can't you be like Martha? Martha's the good girl, Martha's the good student, Martha helps her mom, Martha's the big sister, Martha knows a lot. She can iron a shirt, and she can write an A paper.'"

Her parents were teachers and valued education but told their kids early on that they would have to fund their college tuitions. Martha earned a scholarship, commuted into New York City from Connecticut to attend Barnard College, and modeled in her free time to pay her tuition. Martha Stewart, from a young age, learned to hold traditional femininity and boundless curiosity in equal measures. She could be beautiful and perfect as a sister and daughter and a ferocious student that pushed the boundaries laid before her.

As the oldest of six kids myself, I also read every book I could grab. When I wasn't reading, I played with my brothers and sisters. From age ten, I babysat my younger siblings, who ranged from one to seven years old. Though I wasn't ironing or cooking, I learned early on how to watch out for others before myself. With six kids, four of which were born between 1999 and 2004, there were screams, chases, and bath salons of frothed shampoo and bad French accents. We had Hamburger Helper or chicken and cheesy rice for dinner with little glasses of milk. No cakes except on birthdays. On Mondays, we secured a deal with a local pizza shop: two large pizzas for $20. My mom divided those eight slices in half to make sure there was enough. Our household never worried about a table centerpiece. We worried about having enough. The idea of domesticity for my mom revolved around making sure everything was right for us, her kids. With sports equipment, team practices, school award assemblies, cotillion carpools, and birthday parties, her task of maintaining each of our basic schedules was a full-time job. Each kid had their own schedule of basketball tournaments or school supplies or field trip permission slips or lost shoes, and sometimes, things like a homecoming date's boutonniere wasn't ordered.

"There was always something going on. It felt like things were going a million miles an hour," Mom said. "And sometimes it was too much." It doesn't help that when picking us up from my private Catholic elementary school, she felt the pressure to lose her pregnancy weight within a month or wear tennis whites or Lily Pulitzer to match the other moms on the blacktop where cars idled until classes were dismissed and kids ran outside to go home.

Even today, with my youngest brother soon to be the only one left in the house, there's still pressure on my mom to coordinate all the different pieces of her family's life. Christopher needs gym shorts. Tatum's graduation is coming up. Instead of cooking, my mom orders food from Seamless or Grubhub. My dad jokes if Mom dies, we're screwed because no one knows the passwords to anything—our Verizon account, our streaming accounts, and honestly, who knows what else.

"Do I like cooking?" my mom said. She paused. "No, not really. For so many years, it's something that had to be done. No, I would prefer not to cook. But it's a part of life. I also wouldn't like to do laundry."

The beauty of Martha Stewart comes from the interior décor, frosted cakes, and glossy-paged cookbooks, but she amplifies the beauty by making it seem effortless. She reports her insane routine as if her body gently wakes her at 4 a.m. every day. She is never any emotion but coy (even when talking about her prison stint). She is *ravished* by the monotonous beauty of her uninterrupted routine—though as a mother and a divorcée (or as a human), she may have faced days where she stepped in chicken shit, burned a cake, missed a birthday party, and cried all night. Martha may have even felt anger at the unplanned aggravations of daily life.

Though Martha markets domesticity, she appeals to a utopia where laundry isn't a crippling task that entails days of procrastination, where women can be both domestic and professional without any assistance from other members of their household. If Martha ever appeared anything less than completely satisfied with her life, who would buy the products impersonating answers to the perfectionist desire to have it all?

I can only recall one instance, in a recent interview, where she didn't seem pleasantly at peace with her life. During a Bloomberg panel, the moderator framed a question to Martha by saying everyone in the room wanted to be Martha. "No, they do not," she said. Over the audience's laughter, she says she's joking.

The moderator asks a question, hoping Martha can give expertise to the new marketers in the room. "Do you wish you could do it all again?"

"Um, do I wish? Well in a way yes, of course." Stewart says. "Because then I would be forty years old, and I would be on my way again, and it would be fun."

SPAGHETTI DONUT

When I interned in New York City, Luke came to visit me from Philadelphia, where he lived with his parents after graduation. I dragged him to Smorgasburg, an outdoor food festival, in Brooklyn. We wandered between vendors who were selling chocolate-melted donuts, chili mangoes, and hibiscus lemonade. Full caramelized ducks hung from hooks at one booth. Another vendor had octopus tentacles floating in little soup bowls.

"Ew," Luke said. As someone whose origin involves a three-day hunger strike against eating a dampened PB&J—even though this protest overlapped his birthday and he refused to eat his own cake—Luke has a select palette. No vegetables, no seafood. Indian food, yes. Bacon-egg-cheese breakfast sandwiches (as he pronounces them, "brickfest saammiches"), also yes, almost daily.

Luke looked around and said, "I could see myself living in New York." When I interned in LA, I would talk to Luke about how "my industry" (i.e., entertainment, the industry where I had only completed three undergraduate internships) required me to live in New York or Los Angeles with no flexibility.

Since we've been together, Luke's become more adventurous. Once I said he would never eat escargot at a fancy dinner with his family, and he scooped a snail up from my plate and threw it in his mouth. His mom was shocked. Now, he eats Caesar salads, the gateway into less dairy-based salads.

We both moved to New York City in the fall of 2019, and we grabbed pizza everywhere. We ducked out of our offices and met at the NY Pizza Suprema outside Penn Station on our Friday lunch breaks. We walked into a restaurant for dinner just because it looked nice from the outside. We found diners and split French toast. We ate more pizza, whenever we could, standing on sidewalks and hovering tongue-burning slices over paper plates. I trusted him to dress my pizza with whatever pepper-oregano-parmesan mix he dusted on his own.

When I was unemployed, Luke ordered me endless coffees, sandwiches, and takeout without a single complaint about the cost. I'm employed now, but one night after work, he called and said he would order food if I hadn't eaten anything yet. When I arrived at his place, he had dinner from a Mexican-Indian restaurant we loved and had ordered me a sweet mango lassi just because. He didn't order himself anything because he had already eaten. We cook Hello Fresh meals together and chop whatever vegetables Luke will permit (no carrots, no tomatoes). It is a lot of siracha, lime-zest rice, and pork meatballs, but we review the recipe each time as if it's new.

Sometimes, a meal is just a meal. Each person is going to cook it differently.

Martha Stewart is one household, but not all. My friend Vas, an incredible cook who makes shakshuka or mushroom carbonara for her own curiosity, recognizes that she grew up watching her mom cook; her mom, as an immigrant from India, felt she had to cook Indian meals for her husband and family every week. Vas believes she enjoys cooking while her mom, a good cook, enjoys providing but hates cooking after years of dinner planning. Mikki Kendall in *Hood Feminism* writes mainstream feminism would critique a woman serving a plate to her man, but this white feminist mandate assumes all families hold the same norms. As a Black woman, Kendall writes, "Making a man's plate and other similar practices exist in large part because the only place a Black man might experience respect is from someone in his family."

To think that the only answer to a domestic relationship—one at-home parent, one working parent—is to assume there is only one way for a marriage or partnership to work perfectly.

Alain de Botton in his lecture "Why You Will Marry the Wrong Person" argues that we are guaranteed to marry the wrong person because we don't understand ourselves. We believe that we are perfect partners and a dream to live with, and we expect that our partner will be thrilled to live with us. But sometimes, there's loneliness and misunderstanding in the best relationships. "If your partner can understand sixty percent of your soul, that's great.... Many of the hopes that took you into the marriage will have to die in order for the marriage to continue," de Botton tells Ira Glass on *This American Life*.

There is solitary melancholy within the relationship because we expect the right person to protect us from ourselves. As a married man, de Botton's perspective is somewhat depressing but connected to the unspoken truth of his experience; his own wife wore black at their ten-year wedding anniversary to symbolize the death of her hopes and dreams.

"We are trying to do such a complex thing with someone. We are trying to find our best friend, our ideal sexual partner, our co-household manager, perhaps our co-parent, and we're expecting all this will miraculously go well together. Of course, it can't," de Botton continues, "there will be many areas of misunderstanding and failure."

The failure within a partnership is inevitable. The couples who work the hardest at it won't prevent failures. (My inner perfectionist trembles.) There will be more unhappiness than a married-couple-to-be can predict, and the unhappiness may outweigh the good. So, what can someone do to prepare? Have realistic expectations. "A good partnership," Glass quotes de Botton, "is not so much between two healthy people. There aren't many of those on the planet. It's one between two demented people who have had the skill, or lack, to find a non-threatening conscious combination between the relative insanities. A standard question on a first dinner date should be, 'And how are you crazy?'"

How am I crazy? My other-oriented perfectionism—the shoulds and should nots—allow me to mask how my own rules for a "perfect" relationship confine us. Why do I have to assume that someone has to wear the pants, whether it's me or Luke? Why can't both of us wear...what we want? By fearing and attempting to reverse binding gender roles, I am holding myself and Luke firmly within the limits of "tradition" instead of letting us find our best path forward together.

That day in July 2018, at Smorgasburg, Luke and I bought a spaghetti donut. I took a picture with him holding it, both of us in awe of how two unlikely ingredients could mold together. And honestly? The spaghetti donut? Not that great. It tasted like deep-fried pasta. I don't think either of us would willingly buy one again; we only got it the one time to see what it was like. We walked away from Smorgasburg with the full-stomach satiation of choice, a shared meal where both of us got to choose whatever we wanted.

CHAPTER 7:

THE FUNNY GIRLS

———

Claire Siemietkowski accidentally opened for Jim Gaffigan in February 2020. She didn't know he was in the wings. She didn't even know an A-list comedian was going to be at the same venue. All she knew was she had her own five minutes to perform.

At Gotham Comedy Club in Manhattan, the audience disappeared into the navy darkness as the lights trained on her. Waiters moved between tables. Audience members bit into popcorn shrimp or clinked their beer bottles on table-tops. Otherwise, it was Claire's stage.

She was still new to stand-up comedy, but here she was, at a famed venue with framed photos of a young Jerry Seinfeld, Ellen DeGeneres, and Eddie Murphy greeting guests. Only two months earlier, she had completed a two-week stand-up crash course at Gotham, and the booker pulled her in for a 7 p.m. show.

Most of the other performers were also—or, based on the pauses for laughter or heavy self-deprecation, seemed—new to comedy. One girl joked about being a total freak, but only when it came to making out with strangers at bars. "My

friends over there are laughing because they know it's true!"
she said mid set-up. At this Wednesday show, the audience
responses came from regions of the room as a table of dedicated friends laughed generously where the rest of the audience wouldn't.

Claire stood on stage wearing black clothes and red lip-
stick and performed her set. She talked about a date with a
guy who considered himself a reader because he reads work
emails all-day. "When he went to the bathroom, I Amazon
Primed *Hooked on Phonics* to his apartment," Claire joked.

Her opinion changed when she found out he lived next
door to singer Norah Jones. "I don't care how stupid you are, I
am not going to pass up the opportunity to have Norah Jones
serenade me from her living room window while I fuck this
guy. I imagined after we finished, she would break into her
Grammy-award winning song, 'Come Away With Me'," she
told the audience.

The truth was, Claire revealed to the audience, she didn't
come away with Norah Jones. She came—a little baby Yoda
orgasm—during sex with her lackluster date by imagining
the Popeye's down his street and their new chicken sandwich.
"I've never even had the sandwich, but just thinking about
what it might taste like got me to the finish line faster than
my sexual partner did," she said.

The audience laughed not in polarized regions of oblig-
atory friendship but as one room. As she walked off her set,
wild applause at her back, the host reminded everyone that
they weren't allowed to pull out their phones and welcomed
to the stage a translucently pale Jim Gaffigan—the real deal.

Since Gaffigan's sets never cross beyond a family friendly
rating, his material might have been about zoos. However, it
took a young woman joking about her mediocre sex life to

warm up, or dare I say, lubricate the stage for him to come up, unannounced, and practice new, clean material.

As someone sitting in the show, I was stunned and happy for Claire.

And yet.

There was a part of me that thought, *Sex jokes, really? Claire is too smart to make sex jokes like all the other female comedians.*

Eight months later in quarantine, with live comedy being a distant dream, I ask Claire about this night. I'm wondering whether she hates the trope of women performing sex jokes or not. If people think that female comedians only perform and write raunchy material, what is the responsibility of a female comedian? Wouldn't it be to *not* perform that material and shoot for elevated stuff to show the male haters?

"I struggle doing those kinds of jokes, because I'm like, 'Am I reinforcing a negative pigeon hole for us?'" Claire said. "But then by not doing it, I'm denying my own experiences and my own creativity because those are a lot of the jokes that come naturally to me."

After our interview, she planned on showering and seeing someone she had texted before quarantine. Whatever this date turned into, she already had her mind perked to mine jokes. "If we do hook up tonight, I have jokes to do for my mic tomorrow, like 'Oh, I came out of retirement.' It's just funny, you know?"

**

After so many critics enforcing the trope that "women aren't funny," there is a boldness that comes from the women who do make it to the stage. A boldness that forces the audience to think, listen, and laugh about sexual experiences through the women's perspective. As an audience member, it feels part-culture revolt, part-stubbornness, and part-shock factor. It is an avalanche of sex jokes in a culture that previously ignored female pleasure, orgasms, sexual experiences in hetero relationships. *Listen up, boys,* they say, *you don't have all the answers, and in fact, you might be wrong.*

Now, instead of holding any shock, it is almost expected for female comedians at all levels, open mics or headliners, to find a self-deprecating sex angle. It has become its own trope.

Going through Netflix, I noticed their specials by female comedians poke at sexual innuendos, like Nikki Glaser's *Bangin'* or London Hughes' *To Catch a D*ck.* Netflix advertises Taylor Tomlinson's 2020 special, *Quarter-Life Crisis,* with her comparing herself to Willy Wonka after a guy agrees they can wait to have sex: "Charlie, you won! The factory is for you!" The full special goes into detail about Tomlinson's life, including the fact that she has only slept with two people, one of which was her former fiancé, yet still...the sex jokes steal the show.

I found myself asking the question I found in a Reddit thread, "Any good female comedians that don't only rely on sex jokes and talking trash?" (One user, necrosapien87, commented "Female comedians just do a lot of vagina related material. I wouldn't watch a guy talk about his dick for an hour." So true, necrosapien87.)

The Daily Show correspondent Roy Wood, Jr. explained his stand-up as approaching A-to-C thinking in his comedy around societal issues. "We've argued about A and B on this issue. It's A versus B, it's A versus B. But sometimes there's a C element that you haven't considered. So, with all my comedy I'm just trying to present C and add it to the argument of A and B," Wood, Jr. told Phoebe Robinson on *Sooo Many White Guys.*

When I heard this, I thought, *That's it! Why couldn't more women find an option C, find the original content and stop talking about giving blow jobs?*

The summer I graduated from high school, I watched *Inside Amy Schumer* with my high school boyfriend and scoffed and squirmed at how crude she was. In college, I wrote monologue jokes and sketches for a late-night student show, and I tried my best to make my writing genderless. In 2018, I interned at Upright Citizens Brigade and Comedy Central where my jobs required watching live shows or taped stand-up sets, and I applauded the few women who made the audience laugh without talking about sex at all. They were rare, and there were some sex-adjacent jokes (i.e., Emmy Blotnick suggesting that all the women of the world deserved a "muff dive" from Dwayne "The Rock" Johnson). Those vagina jokes were cooler, more…big picture.

I judged female comedians twice as hard as the path-pavers for me, someone who maybe wanted to pursue comedy myself. If I went into comedy, I would never tell sex jokes, ever. I would use it as satire to a larger political system. I wouldn't waste people's brain space talking about unimportant things like sex! I would be the Wonder Woman of Stand-Up Comedy!

Obviously, the pandemic cancelled any aspiring comedy plans, and live comedy wasn't looking for a Wonder Woman to save the dried-out industry. Yet, in the spring of 2020, I watched comedy specials during work from my parents' guest bedroom, and I couldn't help but wonder, "do women put forward sex jokes because of audience expectations for women, or is it just harder to look for an option C?"

✶✶

After *The New Yorker* and *New York Times* joint investigation on Harvey Weinstein's sexual assault accusations in October 2017, Netflix aired fifty-nine original specials in 2018. Of those, ten featured female headliners (16.9 percent of specials for that year).

However, this number doesn't take into account international specials; if looking exclusively at English-speaking specials that were advertised and promoted in the United States, there were thirty-five specials aired, not fifty-nine. Only five of those English-language specials showcased female comics in an hour-long special: Ali Wong, Tig Notaro, Hannah Gadsby, Ellen DeGeneres, and Iliza Shlesinger. Only five female specials commissioned by Netflix! For reference, John Mulaney has three of his own headliner specials available on the platform. So does Louis C.K.

The optimistic note is that two of the five female comedians were repeat investments for Netflix. Ali Wong and Iliza Shlesinger both had Netflix original specials prior to 2018. In fact, Netflix *loves* Shlesinger. She has aired four original specials and a sketch series through the streaming service since 2015, more than any other female comedian.

One night I came home late from the office, and my roommates were watching Shlesinger's *Freezing Hot*, her first special from 2015—and the third original stand-up comedy special from Netflix ever. ("She's fun, she's sexy, and she's just getting warmed up," the trailer says.) My roommates cracked up at Shlesinger's jokes about liquor goblins and forearm flirting. When whatever spiritual entity assigned gender, Shlesinger jokes, all someone had to do was say fall was their favorite season to be assigned as a girl. "Here's your girl card, here's your Uggs, here's your glitter, now go be insecure, that's what being a girl's all about!" Shlesinger says. One of my roommates laughed and said, "That's so true!"

My mouth had tightened, my forehead scrunched—the opposite of what a comedian hopes to spot from their audience members. *She is just playing on girl stereotypes for an all-girl audience,* I thought. *She's not doing anything new. She's just playing on stuff that seems obvious.* But she's extremely popular with her audience and with Netflix. She's beautiful and feminine but also funny!

Shlesinger embodies this contrast and exhaustion, whether she's aware of the irony or not. Though her comedy comes from her body language that transforms her into goblins, bouncers, or annoying bridesmaids, she wears bronzer contours and crop tops. Her arms are so toned it's borderline an episode of *Friends.* No matter what character she is in, she has to look beautiful. This contrast—the funny and the sexy in one space, at last!—is on the home page of her website. Her most recent advertisement for her wedding-oriented special, *Unveiled,* is an anime Shlesinger in a ripped bridal dress rising out of flames with balloon tits, a Barbie waist, and a satisfied smirk. A comic of a comic. A caricature of a masculine idea of a funny gal.

**

"Do you know how many sex robot jokes there are out there? So. Many. So many guys have sex robot jokes, and I have robot jokes that aren't about sex, so that makes me different," Kasha Patel said.

Kasha claims she is the funniest Indian female comic from West Virginia, period. Surprisingly, she started while in the science journalism graduate program at Boston University. She went to open mics with science jokes, but they didn't seem to work. Instead, she started with jokes about dating in her twenties. "The easiest thing in comedy to write about is yourself," Patel said. "That's why everyone's first special, it's always about themselves and growing up. You see that in Kevin Hart, George Carlin. But then when they get older and they get that up out of their system, they start being able to comment on things that are more personal to them."

When she moved to DC to work for NASA, she decided to write more jokes about science than her personal life. She translated scientific discoveries in lay terms by day, then she made the translations funny at nightly open mics. As a hybrid between a scientist and a comedian, Kasha created a ratio to measure the success of her jokes. If she compared the seconds it took to deliver the joke set-up and punchline to the seconds of audience laughter, she could find a ratio to quantify the success of her jokes. This is the beauty of a scientist comedian, someone who applies structure to the abstractly subjective.

For Kasha, stand-up material comes down to voice, but voice can take years to find itself. "New comics, whether they are female, male or whatever—they all have sex jokes," Patel said. "There's so many females in the comedy scene in D.C. that have like these really grotesque sex jokes, and I'm like, wow, that's a lot, but I think when you advance, and you get better at writing material, you can stray away from those things."

What drew me to Kasha was her perfect mix of her interests. She loves science, and she loves comedy, and she mixes them together both at work and at nightly open mics. She didn't write what the audience expected (cough, cough, blow job jokes) and created a unique identity to tackle important issues through comedy. She created an option C.

After talking to Kasha, it seemed like every comedian has to get through their personal phase of easy-topic jokes (sex/dating, drugs, childhood/family) to reach the elevated and necessary point of social commentary.

Jenny Yang, one of *Vulture's* 2020 Comics to Watch, told Bitch Media that comedy helped her recover from her perfectionism. However, that freedom to be imperfect doesn't mean people can walk up to their first open mic and expect to tackle the heavy societal issues. "Anything that's taboo or that's tough to talk about in polite conversation, if a comic wants to talk about it, it's like handling radioactive energy," Yang said. "If you are not skilled enough to handle it, then you're gonna fucking die. You're gonna fuck it up for yourself, and people are gonna hate you. That's what's gonna happen."

The same way that a student doesn't operate a buzzsaw unchaperoned on their first day in woodshop (and my experience with woodshop is '90s sitcoms), a rookie comic doesn't try to tackle politics, rape culture, and genocide in their first five-minute set at an open mic.

We expect that any comedian will clear a pathway of representation, and that burden falls doubly hard on any comedian who is not a straight white male. That comedian has to deliver an enlightenment to help everyone see and navigate the complex world we live in.

Tanael Joachim, a Haitian immigrant and comedian, faced a heckler in response to a #MeToo joke. The joke? "Matt Lauer pulled his dick out at work and that cost him a $26 million job. Some people do the same thing on the subway, and it only costs them $2.75."

A man in the audience yelled at Joachim to say that he was defending sexual assault, and Joachim argued otherwise: "Sifting through the righteous anger, two related and recurring trends become apparent: First, the practice of holding others to an impossible standard of ideological purity, and second, the practice of advertising one's own moral superiority. Neither of these practices has any basis in reality because we all have flaws we strive to keep hidden, and no matter how ferociously we denounce our neighbor, we are all only one unguarded remark from a public shaming."

We all want other people to say the right thing, so when people start talking about taboo subjects—even if the taboo is under the common topic of sex and dating—other people want to prove that they are *not* siding with controversy.

So, if I am resistant to female comedians talking about their bodies, their sex lives, or their femininity at all, what does that say about *me*?

**

Through cooking, I have explored how other-oriented perfectionism impacts a perfectionist's interpersonal relationships and how reality competitions and troll culture welcomes expertise from fans with less-than-beginner skills.

Hypothetically, would providing social commentary on an underrepresented demographic from someone within the demographic (i.e., me, a woman, talking about other women) be less troll-ish and more empowering? Am I inflicting high standards on others, or am I recognizing the societal norms that would hold any of us back on stage? If I debate the most impactful content for female comedians, is that activism or perfectionism?

In the 1930s, Alfred Adler connected superiority and perfectionism. Adler observed how people sought to improve themselves to reframe their reputation from negatively to positively perceived. "This is the individual's creative and compensatory answer to the normal and universal feelings of insignificance and disempowerment, and the accompanying beliefs that one is less than what one should be (i.e., feelings of inferiority)," Richard E. Watts write about Adler's discovery. To prevent feelings of inferiority, the perfectionist positions themselves as superior.

Adler believed that the perfectionist striving could be beneficial or self-serving depending on the communal benefit. He labeled "striving for perfection" as a horizontal approach that sought to raise the individual alongside their community. Striving stepped into narcissism when someone strived for "superiority," a position that allowed themselves to look down on their peers within their community. Adler suggested that the horizontal approach that considered the common good and the community led to healthier perspectives.

In looking down on female comedians for sex jokes, am I pushing those comedians to be perfect? Or am I establishing myself as their moral superior to allow myself to feel better, different, and special?

Shlesinger, the party goblin and the only female comedian with four Netflix specials, said in a 2017 *Deadline* interview that women needed to stop talking about their vaginas and come up with something more original. Shlesinger said,

I could walk into The Improv [in LA], close my eyes, and I can't tell one girl's act apart from another. That's not saying that thirty-something white guys don't all sound the same sometimes, but I'm banging my head against the wall because

women want to be treated as equals, and we want feminism to be a thing, but it's really difficult when every woman makes the same point about her vagina, over and over. I think I'm the only woman out there that has a joke about World War II in my set.

This superiority sounds familiar, yes?

Other women in comedy responded to Shlesinger saying that she was

1. hypocritical because her material also involved vaginas (including dressing as a vagina in her ABC Family sketch show)
2. tearing down the limited pool of aspiring and professional female comedians
3. looking to affirm she's "different than other comics"
4. not cool for having a World War II joke as her most contemporary current event

It is important to note that Shlesinger's career came from making universal appeals to women. Then she turned on women for being too basic. A *Vulture* article quoted Laurie Kilmartin, a *Conan* writer, and her Twitter thread responding to Shlesinger's comments.

Early in my career I also wanted to be THE female comic that changed men's minds about women. Then I realized there were tons of...

Funny women and it didn't matter to sexist men if I was funny. They remained their awful selves.

Trying to "change minds" is exhausting. It will break you, one day, because it's an unattainable goal.

One of the many, many sentences Shlesinger posted then deleted in response to the backlash read, "How's this— instead of thinking because you're a girl that you can just yell 'pussy' and think it's a revelation, try doing better and working harder. That's all there is to it...I am your champion, and you can't see beyond your own Twitter thread. My book #girlLogic is out in November. It will be out and so will a new Netflix special, celebrating women." It's like *Lean In,* but for comedy.

Shlesinger, as a woman in comedy, has faced her own level of resistance. She understands the misogyny that exists and wants females to step above the critics' ammunition. *Be so good they can't boo you.* But her statement actually boos all the other women for getting on stage and not doing things the Shlesinger way. It also welcomes boos from the trolls who would already think that women aren't anything but sex jokes—if a female comedian said it, it must be a real problem, right?

Adler's definition of striving for perfection originated over a century ago. Perfectionism was, and still is, new territory for psychologists, but I love that his *striving for perfection* involved an individual seeking to better themselves and pull their community up with them. The irony of perfectionism today is in the wealth of voices and platforms available, a perfectionist has to focus on promoting themselves to be heard above the din.

When someone like Shlesinger, or myself, steps on a soap-box to tell other people what they can and can't do, it's not about whether the audience follows orders as much as it is about that time in the spotlight, on the soapbox, practicing a tight five of internalized misogyny.

**

I have a confession.
I have ten minutes of stand-up material.
From that, I have a few jokes I love.

1. I'm the oldest of six kids, so I was young enough to watch trailers saying, "coming soon, *Dora the Explorer!*" and watched that show long enough to think, "When is this bitch going to lose The Map and get a GPS?"
2. I trusted Elmo with everything. He taught me to read, to share, and to trust that the creepy white man dancing outside my window was probably Mr. Noodle's brother, Mr. Noodle.
3. Going to an all-girls Catholic school, I flirted like a nun. I touched boys' elbows and asked how their parents were doing.

...Maybe you just had to be there. I swear, I crushed it for at least two seven-person audiences.

There was one other raunchy joke I love. It came halfway off-the-cuff after a too-long story publicly shaming my friend about not knowing how to find his girlfriend's clitoris. As the audience went stiff, I stopped and said:

1. Is that too much, boys? You guys think you're Christopher Columbus of the female body? Well, Christopher Columbus ended up in the wrong *continent*.

A college freshman came up to me after the show and said her mom laughed really hard at that one.

It made me feel cool, like I said something that mattered. I cherished that I made that mother-daughter relationship a little more awkward. Though it wasn't a Shlesinger World War II joke, it felt contemporary to have a crowd laugh back and along with me.

Here is the truth of the situation. In a world of option A or option B, here is my option C.

For me, sex—perhaps because of the Catholic upbringing of both shame and tradition, perhaps because of learning sex through male partners who knew what they wanted when I didn't—was never for me. In my monogamist history, sex made me satisfied if it pleased my partner. I wanted to be someone else's perfect attraction. If I wasn't, it felt like a personal failure, though circumstances—as with any sexual interaction—carry more nuance than A or B.

I remember watching all this sex-positive comedy content of women having orgasms and changing their life, and I defensively thought, *What is the big deal with this? It's just sex.*

A few months ago, I went to schedule a gynecology appointment on a Planned Parenthood website, and they listed "female orgasm disorders" as a condition they treated.

I had never heard this phrase before in my life. Whiskey dick? Erectile dysfunction? In college, these things came up, some might say, too much in dinner conversation. No girls ever talked about orgasms—if they were having them, if they weren't, how they were communicating with their partner about it, what it felt like. I assumed that having sex alone was fine. I never realized, or considered, my own sexual enjoyment with any partner I ever had.

When I heard women create these jokes or web series around discovering orgasms, part of me probably resented them as a perfectionist. *You don't have to have an orgasm to become a full woman. There are so many bigger, better things to discuss like climate change* (which is as popular to discuss in comedy as World War II).

Months before this, on the cusp of me moving from Manhattan to DC to survive the apocalyptic pandemic phase with my family, Luke and I went to see Jacqueline Novak's one-woman show *Get On Your Knees.* She talked about blowjobs—but that's not it. She talked about the fragility of the male ego and the gentle vulnerability of the penis reflected through its name (she notes "nis" as the ignored syllable that softens the organ into a deflated hiss, a wilting flower). She talked about the fear of being bad at blowjobs in high school, then of considering blowjobs as a generous gift to her college peers. She talked about authenticity, life, death, cave people, boyfriends' fathers, poetry. She spoke like a bard on the teenage experience of finding sexuality and sexual reputation's boundaries.

"An overthinker's delight, and a reminder that a woman's humor can cut as deeply as her rage," *The New Yorker* wrote in its review.

At the end of the show, my jaw dropped open. "Wow," I said to Luke, though I was slightly worried that he would say the show had been too girly, too feminine. *It's too girly for a guy to get,* I thought.

But it wasn't. Luke liked it. It allowed us both to connect as we talked about her words, her experiences. We talked about our previous relationships. I felt like he could maybe get some perspective that he wouldn't find otherwise through a stranger's monologue about a toothy blowjob. He could understand something I understood alongside Novak without my having to explain for myself the power dynamics of oral sex. We both laughed a lot. It is a touch stone for both of us. In reading an early version of this chapter, Luke said, "I think it's missing something. Your option C. Get on your knees."

My option C turned out to be that I was a perfectionist, even when it came to my sex life, that instead pointed at the reputational needs of female sexuality. "We are more than our bodies" is an easy picket sign when I was, and am, scared of my own body. My perfectionism has definitely influenced the orgasm disorder. I have run a spiel for a few sex therapists over introductory phone calls. For me, I can't connect the scientific with the subjective. I can articulate my trauma in the frame of my body or my shame, but the biology and mentality are disconnected. Perhaps there is something physically wrong with me that my inner perfectionist is dying to fix. I probably don't think I deserve it. I probably am still carrying my trauma. I probably am still thinking, "Who cares? What's the big deal with all this vagina talk?"

Isn't this the same thing I do at comedy shows? Run mental notes through each comedians' jokes? The best part about a comedy show is the versatility. Each comedian is different, even if they all talked about the weather. Even if you saw the same comedian twice in one week, they might change their set. Do the sets have to be perfect? Isn't there also some beauty in watching someone tweak a joke or acknowledge a silent response when the audience doesn't laugh? Isn't the risk of neither party predicting what the other will do part of the excitement?

Maybe—just maybe—sex and comedy sets are both better when you sit back, stop thinking, and allow yourself to laugh.

CHAPTER 8:

THE CITY BLUEPRINT

———

would love to stay in tonight & watch a movie. maybe order some dumplings. just take it easy. unfooooortunately, that would feel like "wasting my 20s" and "missing out on life" so i will instead stop by three parties in opposite parts of town one of which i need a costume for <3

—CALEB HEARON (@CALEBSAYSTHINGS)

ON TWITTER, JUNE 12, 2021

A used, naked twin mattress and my roommate's fan occupied ninety percent of my floor space in my first Manhattan apartment. That summer, I sat at my parents' home with a master's degree, reading books and crying about job applications. That fall, I was in the city that made people. The ceiling above my head lifted, and I considered every possibility of who I could be. I could sneak away to open mics late after work and return while my roommates slept. I could watch every movie in theaters during award season. I could wake up at 5 a.m. like famous writers said they did in their day job phases. These options were too glamorous to consider while lounging on my parents' patio. *Not now,* I thought, *but then, in the city of artists.*

I came to New York for an imagined badge of honor. I signed a lease before an offer letter. I wanted the grit of tight monthly finances at a job that would undervalue and overwork me. I interviewed at a small talent agency representing Broadway and screen actors. I told the CEO my biggest weakness was that I was a perfectionist, and he laughed.

"So, you do things too well?" he joked.

"It doesn't always help me, though," I said. "It means I'm triple checking things, and I think I need to figure out a way to make sure everything is right without taking too much time." A promise to be more efficient, to check harder than before.

I took my first job, a minimum wage biweekly paycheck that covered less than my rent and focused on my cultural education. I would be that person that quotes *The New Yorker* and reads books pre-bestseller list on the subway and explores a new neighborhood each Saturday to learn Manhattan. People would think I was cultured, well-read, and super smart. I'd be a city girl with an encyclopedic mind that inventoried random tips like the best neighborhood coffee and intellectual opinions on foreign policy.

Instead, I snoozed my writing alarms in the mornings and spent an hour arranging my six clothing items into a new outfit. I spent lunches studying Hemingway and memoirs while watching the microwave clock. After work, I walked to the movies, traveled to Luke's apartment in Jersey City, got drinks with someone in the city, went to a comedy show, or grabbed a French vanilla coffee from the coffee machine in my apartment's lounge to engineer plot into my thesis short stories. Rarely did I step back into my apartment before 10 p.m.

That's how I could measure my time in the city, by the hours outside my apartment. Because each day felt like it could be special—dinner in a new restaurant, beer with an old friend—I had to make it special. I could not waste any days in this new city. When my family asked if I liked it "up there," my memorized response was "You can run around and find something to do on, like, a Wednesday." I paused as if considering Wednesday, but I always said Wednesday.

When my college friends flocked to the same bar with beer buckets and fried pickles for Saturday football games, part of me felt disgusted. In a city of new places, repeated attendance was a time waste. *I should be exploring a new neighborhood every weekend to learn about Manhattan.* I could dissect the city into neighborhoods, find the best restaurants and parks within those neighborhoods, and fine-comb Manhattan until I knew a little bit of everything.

The idea of studying the island gave me a slight schoolgirl rush. My lack of follow-through on my ideas about examining each street of Manhattan, especially when I agreed to social plans that involved bars full of college students, was frustrating. As my own teacher and student, I disappointed myself on both sides of the educational relationship.

The Manhattan I moved to versus the Manhattan I expected also shifted my expectations. Based on movies I watched, New York City was where the toughest went to prove they had the grit to survive anything—and then crushed the city in their palm with their success. Today's Manhattan caters to the post-grad crowd and welcomes them like Regina George's mom in *Mean Girls,* offering snacks and condoms in a desperate ploy for youthful attention.

When I moved in, the Financial District streets blurred with suits power-walking into tall brick buildings and other post-college kids hustling to a morning commute. My friends and I ordered Ubers before considering subway maps on the weekends. My Instagram showed more and more people from my hometown posing in SoHo or Williamsburg, biding those few pre-marriage years in their twenties before they planned to return to our parents' neighborhoods. New York City was not the cutthroat competition of rom-coms or cable Christmas movies that harden people's souls against their hometowns! It was not the struggling-artist utopia of beatniks and epiphanies! It was a retreat for twenty-somethings. An expensive one.

The bohemian idea of New York, of artistic grit and Beatnik poets, disappeared to accommodate Trader Joe's and white-walled coffee shops.

In graduate school, we read Patti Smith's *Just Kids* and analyzed Smith and Robert Mapplethorpe's oath to an artistic life through their collection of silver skulls, the constant consumption of poetry, and their room at Hotel Chelsea. They had nothing but a rented studio space. "We gathered our colored pencils and sheets of paper and drew like wild, feral children into the night, until, exhausted, we fell into bed," Smith writes. To disappear into art in the city that provided the fodder, the visual and intellectual nutrients for a day of primal scribbling, and the recluse: this is the New York I wanted.

Reading the pages from a sidewalk-friendly college town, I could provide the ointment for the pain I felt around my own writing, the failure of a daily practice, the doubt in the words. I'd find my female, platonic Mapplethorpe. A Fey to a Poehler. An Abbi to an Ilana. With her, I would have permission and space to write. With her, I could escape myself and find a community.

Both the teacher and student within me clucked their tongues. *It's too easy,* I thought. *None of us would've survived old New York.*

**

New York is the most American city. That's not a New York resident's hyperbole of New York. When people picture the land where you can "make it there, make it anywhere," the most American of dreams, they picture skyscrapers blocking the sun on the sidewalk while ambulances and taxis wail. It is tall buildings with impressive corporate titles. It is people of all backgrounds and journeys arriving on the same sidewalks to passively power-walk around tourists.

As Amy Plitt and Raven Snook clearly outline, it's a city of contradictions. "You can grab a slice for a buck at any number of pizza joints all over Manhattan, but you might pay upwards of $3,000/month to rent an apartment on the island," they write. It is historic yet modern, stressful yet beautiful. In January, I walked into a millions-of-dollars apartment (washer/dryer, two bedroom, fifteen-foot ceilings) that my friend had found through a family friend whose parents had bought the unit "discounted" in the pandemic. To reach the apartment from Union Square, I walked around scattered paper plates, orange peels, abandoned black sneakers, and a soft roll of feces leaning against the wall below the firework where it had been (presumably, anally) propelled.

"That's amazing! A human shit!" two androgynous characters said walking ahead of me on the subway, as if they spotted a polar bear in Antarctica, a fable incarnate.

It is easy for me to think that I'm different than the humans marveling at shit or moving into a nice apartment sponsored by familial financial support. While I paid my own bills for my twin-bedroom-turned-office, I also escaped New York during the pandemic. I returned home to DC, where my mom did my laundry and my dad made spaghetti. I paid rent in Manhattan and lived in the suburbs. When people talk about New York bouncing back post-pandemic, I am the one who bounced and returned, a prodigal daughter with loyalty to comfort over instability.

Though I feared the reality of the coronavirus sweeping New York, I held onto the idea of the city during the pandemic. I re-signed my lease in July a few days after my company furloughed me. Financially, not a sound decision. I sent all my unemployment checks back to the Financial District, where I wasn't living, to soothe myself that I could go back, if I wanted, when the time arose. (Read: "the time" meaning when the city was no longer ravaged by COVID-19 while I kept tabs from another state.)

As a perfectionist, I wanted New York City to not only meet my high standards (self-realization, complete community) but also provide the spark to finally metamorphize into the perfect version of myself (more cultured/intelligent/well-spoken/creative/generous/woke/philanthropic).

Ironically, I thought New York would have a blueprint for the non-traditional life I abstractly wanted.

**

In 2001, Richard Florida, an urban studies theorist, walked along Carnegie Mellon's campus. He met a young man with spiked rainbow hair, piercings, and tattoos. Florida assumed he was a rock star, but the student was an engineer being recruited for a company in Austin.

Florida asked this man why not stay in Pittsburgh? There were internationally renowned museums and three professional sports teams. The student said he wanted to move away from Pittsburgh to Austin: "How would I fit in here?"

Florida's study on the "creative class"—young post-college employees whose jobs generate creativity through problem-solving, whether that's engineers, financial analysts, professors, or painters, and who "share a common ethos that values creativity, individuality, difference, and merit"—suggested that cities needed to attract this creative class in order to grow their economies.

A company could plant their headquarters in a city like 2001 Pittsburgh with its museums and sports venues, but if the creative class couldn't detect outdoor activity options, street-level restaurants and cafes, a thriving nightlife, and a hum of social tolerance in a historic place filled with other (young) creative class members, they wouldn't bite.

Creative classes were drawn to the same cities that had a large openly gay population, measured through Gary Gates's originally named "Gay Index," and Florida's Bohemian Index, measuring writers' and artists' moves to cities.

To summarize, Florida hypothesized that the creative class would flock to a city if it had:

- diversity in population, not only along ethnic, racial, or background differences but in thought
- new types of music and food to explore
- a varied nightlife, even if the creative class member personally will not partake ("another signal that a city 'gets it,'" Florida quips)
- active participation in the creative class's own stimulation

- natural landmarks that allow physical and natural activities like running, biking, or even, for the adventurous, kayaking…or snowboarding (if you're one of those)
- an authenticity that comes from the exposed brick of historical landmarks

Looking at it, I recognize myself studying neighborhood walks to "stumble upon" a restaurant or bookstore as if it was as casual as a webpage. A massive checklist of what the city must provide for someone seeking creativity. For the creative class who honor individuality and new answers, there is a generic checklist that boils down their interests and can place them in any growing city in the United States, maybe the world.

"They want to pack their time full of dense, high-quality, multidimensional experiences. Seldom has one of my subjects expressed a desire to get away from it all. They want to get into it all, and do it with eyes wide open," Florida writes.

There's a perfectionist angle to this: try, then enjoy, everything. When paralyzed with worrying about choosing the wrong path in life, stick a foot in every metaphorical door. Take improv classes at night. Do Orange Theory or Rumble or SoulCycle in the morning before work. Flick through all Hinge options. Explore a new coffee shop. Reserve a table for bottomless brunch on Saturday at a new spot to expand conversational restaurant knowledge. Visit the landmarks, both the natural ones like Central Park and the consumer ones like flagship stores.

With the option to try everything, there is always the whisper that the best spot, the hole-in-the-wall place that serves imposter syndrome antidotes and a homelike comfort, is around the corner.

Michael Brustein, a clinical psychologist in Manhattan, told *The Atlantic* that his New York clients have faced increasing perfectionism since he started practicing in 2007. "You're in New York because you're ambitious, you have this need to strive," he says. "But then your whole identity gets wrapped into a goal." It would make sense that this work hard/play hard clientele applies the same goal-setting mindset from their career to their leisure.

When Luke visited me the summer I interned in Manhattan, I planned the entire trip. On Friday, when he came in, he met my friend Lucy. On Saturday, we woke up early to go to Smorgasburg and eat spaghetti donuts. At night, we went to dinner at Carmine's, the Italian restaurant in Times Square, and walked around, bathed in white light from glowing advertisements.

Everything was planned and boiled down to a nice list, "a good weekend in New York City."

Living in a city, or rather expressing how well someone knows a city with brunch or tourist recommendations, becomes a signal. How well do you know the city? Are you cultured enough, in conversation, to know the current spots that someone else could take their mom or their best friend? (There is also something imposterishly perfectionist about having to prove to others that you deserve to call the place you pay to live a home.) One friend at dinner the other night admitted she checks restaurants' Instagram tags to find crowdsourced reviews of the best drinks and meals a restaurant had to offer. If there is only one chance to be at a restaurant before moving onto the next, then even something as simple as a cocktail order better be "the best." She wanted to make sure she maximized her order at this restaurant, but she was also partially embarrassed she admitted that she sourced other people's opinions at all.

In *Can't Even,* Anne Helen Petersen describes this anxiety in appearing culturally in touch, "To be cultured is to be culturally omnivorous, no matter how much time it takes…when you only have so much time to dedicate to leisure, there's a constant demand to make the very best use of your time, consuming the products and engaging in leisure that most effectively demonstrates your status as a cultural omnivore."

Even in leisure moments, there has to be a productive angle. The experience has to add to our conversational repertoire, even if the stores—national chains that imitate the cozy aesthetic of a mom-and-pop shop—that move in alongside the post-college population are as generic as your hometown's McDonald's, Starbucks, and Sweetgreen.

We like what we know. What if any city could become familiar, filled with your favorite stores? What if New York, the city of all cities, actually became one of many replicated cities?

**

My friend Laura, a fresh resident of Pittsburgh, and I were talking about this, and she said, "So, this might be getting into my own research, but Pittsburgh's urban planning department has made a concerted effort over the years to make the city like a more affordable New York. There's an emphasis on small, local restaurants, and Southside has more bars per acre than anywhere else in the world. I sound like I'm defending it (lol), but this is to say that the reputation of the city (like NYC's) sometimes holds more weight for real estate costs than anything else."

Then she sent me an article with the headline, "Could the Next Brooklyn Be Pittsburgh?"

Laura has a great point and one I want to underline. Any city can appeal to the creative class, who have the budget for higher rent buildings being erected and can bring in more commercial real estate, by taking Florida's suggestions. Florida even started a city planning consulting group called "The Creative Class Group" that caters to cities that want to cater to the creative class. These real estate trends that make a contemporary city create a blanket formula for all major or developing cities in America, from San Francisco to Charlottesville, Virginia. They can all be the same.

While I can talk about New York as someone living in New York City, my friends across the country are having this same experience of exploratory motivation: *move to a new place that is your own while you can (or, rather, before a kid or partner makes your choices for you).*

When I lived in Los Angeles, my roommates and I planned our weekends around squeezing out all the juice in this city. We visited the Getty Museum, Malibu beach, Runyon Canyon, and any restaurant that fell under "best pizza LA" on Google searches. Living in a city creates opportunities, and a new anything can be found on Instagram, a *Thrillist* "best of" article, or a word-of-mouth recommendation.

New York City is not alone in rolling out red carpets in a strip of fresh-faced restaurants, comedy theaters, and local breweries to appeal to the post-grad creative class. In my trips to Denver, Nashville, Philadelphia, Baltimore, and even my hometown of DC, there are recognizable chains that grow around the post-grad creative class, like juice bars or cycling boutiques.

To elaborate on the universality of contemporary cities, one of my friends in Seattle asked a group chat for new recipe recommendations because she needed to shop outside Trader Joe's frozen dumplings. The chat, consisting of high school friends that now live in Chicago, Austin, New York, or DC, all responded with their Trader Joe's recommendations, a chain that brought us together nationwide.

We don't all go to New York for that "get-away-from-home" experience. In fact, another important point Florida makes is that there are more creative class members because millennials who grew up in the rise of the creative class are getting married later. Expanded singlehood allows more young employees to explore features of their new cities. The twenties are now reserved for self-exploration in building the foundation of who you will become.

Meg Jay, a clinical psychologist, talks about how twenty-somethings procrastinate life planning. She talks about one of her therapy patients who didn't understand why she, the patient, wasn't married with kids in her dream job by thirty. Jay realized that this patient spent her twenties assuming nothing counted, avoiding making lasting relationships or networking within her job. The patient assumed those years were for making mistakes and learning, but they were actually "the defining decade" that would determine how the rest of her life would go.

"Make no mistake," Jay says. "The stakes are very high."

Jay's book, *The Defining Decade: Why Your Twenties Matter and How to Make the Most of Them Now*, was published in April 2012, almost a decade ago. In the decade to follow, this idea of maximizing your twenties would become mainstream.

At twenty-five, most of my friends are in long-term relationships, live in a new city, have steady and impressive jobs, and fill their free time with hobbies. Some are completing graduate school, and some have very comfortable salaries in tech.

Despite this perceived success, most of us have some level of productivity anxiety when it comes to free time. My friend Erica (who lives in Boston) told me that she does three Peloton rides a week, started tennis lessons, and revived her old skiing habit this past winter. She and her roommate also curate a cooking TikTok and prioritize traveling on their weekends.

Everyone fears that they are going to live their twenties wrong—especially if compounded with the uterine fear of missing the window to have kids or a marriage before thirty-five. We spent our lives shooting for checkpoints in our grades or extracurriculars or program acceptances to let us know we were doing something right. Now we are adults with no guidelines for how to live "right." As a generation being raised with perfectionist standards, we seek a non-existent validation outside of ourselves to prove we won't have regrets—that we will have, indeed, lived a perfect life.

As Anne Helen Petersen writes in her viral article on millennials as the burnout generation,

I laughed at the eternal refrain—*These younger kids, what dorks, we were way cooler*—but not until I returned to campus years later as a professor did I realize just how fundamentally different those students' orientation to school was. There were still obnoxious frat boys and fancy sorority girls, but they were far more studious than my peers had been. They skipped fewer classes. They religiously attended office hours. They emailed at all hours. But they were also anxious grade grubbers, paralyzed at the thought of graduating, and regularly stymied by assignments that called for creativity. They'd been guided closely all their lives, and they wanted me to guide them as well. They were, in a word, *scared*.

There's a tension between the apparent freedom of choice to the creative class and the limitations of youth. Someday, their time in the city will dissolve like fairy dust and leave the creative class blinking their crow's feet and catching passing glimpses of themselves in a neon jumpsuit that sags and looks garishly out-of-date.

Someone can have the flexibility to be who they are, but only as a young professional. The city will bend the rules, but when the thirties come, get your engagement rings and crying babies and make room for the next round of gentrifiers.

How can we know what we're doing is right? That we're living the right lives for ourselves?

**

From his bike ride across America, cross-country cyclist and philanthropist Leo Walsh remembers two difficult moments: a near-death dehydration in a California desert relieved by a standalone gas station and the day his family and friends stood on the lawn of his parents' house to send him off.

Leo is a mover. When we played capture the flag together as kids, no one could catch Leo (it was a pain in the ass to be on the other team, especially since most of us were vertically stunted by pre-puberty). His cross-country bike ride with Peace Players, a non-profit that connects communities through basketball, was his third nomadic trip in four years. In 2017, he spent a year living in a new international country each month. In 2018, he traveled the United States and

Canada, living out of his car and documenting basketball hoops through his Instagram account @peachbaskets.

By May 2020, in the crux of the pandemic's ominous loom and Black Lives Matter protests, Leo wanted to find a way to give back. He had followed people who had traveled across the country on social media and held onto the idea for a while. As the world adapted to a longer-term remote workplace, Leo decided this was the time to go.

People have asked Leo about the hardest part of his trip, but no one asked him what the most difficult part was about preparing to leave. When he told his parents about the bike ride, he watched their faces cloud with fear.

"I told my mom to her face that I was going to do this thing, and she was convinced I was going to die," Leo told me. "And I was going to do it anyway."

Leo planned the trip for a net-positive impact. Though he wanted to do the trip, he oriented it around serving local communities by partnering with a non-profit. "I thought I was doing it for—like, it's not going to affect anyone. No one else is doing it. I'm going to do it."

On the day he left home, his friends traveled to see him off, and he reconsidered how intertwined he was to the people he loved, to his Scranton hometown. "Why am I leaving this? Why am I moving away from all this love?" Leo said. "So, I was slapped in the face with how good of a life I have, that I'm leaving, leading up to the trip."

Later, when Leo came out of his two days in the desert and collapsed in a gas station by the refrigerated beverages with four demolished water bottles crushed around him, he checked his phone. His older sister had sent a picture of his one-year-old nephew to their family chat, and he almost cried.

"I really didn't realize what that was doing to other people around me," Leo said.

Leo hasn't considered himself a perfectionist, and I would classify him more as a stoic. He accepts that he was the only one in his family to get turned down from Boston College, where his four siblings attended. He doesn't hold onto job rejections as a reflection of his worth. In fact, in my mind, Leo Walsh seemed to operate outside of anyone's expectations at all. I swore I would throw my laptop and phone out the window and travel—in the middle of writing this book—to escape and see things and explore like Leo did, but...I never did. I stayed where I was, whether that was my Manhattan apartment or my parents' house.

Talking to Leo made me realize that even if I hypothetically stopped prioritizing what people thought—or went off the grid, inaccessible to anyone else's obligations—my impact doesn't disappear. Instead, I have the communities I carry with me, my family and friends who will continue to be attached to me, and the direct environment, from my unseen neighbors to the tree planted outside my building with a popped unicorn balloon caught in its branches.

Jenny Odell in her book *How to Do Nothing: Resisting the Attention Economy* argues that social media giants like Twitter, Instagram, and Facebook profit from disrupting the attention of their users. Instead of seeking context to current events, they engage with inflammatory content that provokes them to anger and results in more shares (and more profit for the company itself). These online communities hinge their connection on rage or fear. Her antidote suggests doing nothing: rebuild personal attention spans as if tending to an atrophied muscle and look at the world around you. Notice it. See the birds and trees you walk past every day without thinking twice about them. Feel a connection to them not as accessories or props in your setting but as other living creatures.

She references Sarah Schulman's book *Gentrification of the Mind: Witness to a Lost Immigration,* a memoir about living in New York City as a lesbian during the AIDS epidemic. As queer men died, white suburban kids, the offspring of the "white flight" to the suburbs, moved into these apartments.

As this white suburban community filled the literal spaces left by the dying queer community, Schulman watched as the queer community's history of rebellion embedded in these neighborhoods also disappeared. New gentrifying businesses ("beacons that signaled to newcomers using aesthetics and price") created a universal culture while erasing the effort of the gay community in the Lower East Side.

"Afraid of anyone who differed from the suburban archetype, the newcomers to Schulman's neighborhood were not only uninterested in learning anything about the incredibly dynamic place they had moved to, but ignorant of their role in destroying that dynamism," Odell summarizes.

Florida, in his retrospect of his own work, condemns gentrification, though the creative class appeal does appeal to this white, well-paid group that wants lower rent in a city-adjacent neighborhood starting to turn out its long-standing residents.

"What gives cities their special economic and cultural energy is their diversity of people and economic functions— the way they push people of different ethnicities, incomes, cultures, races, educations, and interests into close proximity, enabling them to interact and combine and recombine in unique and powerful ways. While our cities may be increasingly diverse in terms of nationality, ethnicity, and sexual orientation, they are becoming ever-more divided by class," Florida wrote about the creative class's expansion and New York gentrification in *Bloomberg CityLab*. Likewise, Odell advises that citizens need to engage with their local communities as a form of activism. Engaging with the contemporary and pre-existing history of the areas where we live allows us to see the context of where we stand in our communities, physically and chronologically. Odell believes that a world marked by efficiency allows citizens to render "ineffective" creatures—pigeons, trees grown in street medians, invisible neighbors only heard through a wall—as unnecessary. However, this hurts the local community and ourselves.

There is no way to live a "right" life. However, it is easy to see any city as "a city" as the real estate starts to blur each area's unique identities. How is New York different from Miami or Los Angeles or Dallas if the same corporate chains exist in all places? The question comes down to history influencing the current population and local political issues. Taking the time to notice the world around us, from basketball hoops to birds to stray cats to local trees, is at least a way to anchor us to where we are. Instead of asking how the city can serve my needs to maximize my twenties, how can I engage with this place to make it into a home for others and myself?

**

When I sat in expensive pubs watching the football team I used to root for in the stands, my skin crawled. Every weekend in New York, before the pandemic, was an opportunity cost. I could do the formulaic thing, half-watch football while smothering my face in some buffalo chicken equivalent like I had programmed myself to do for four years of Saturdays before this, or I could be doing...something else. *But what?* I didn't know. But now, I might?

The world is re-opening from the pandemic's lockdown, and I can feel that same itch to checkout all restaurants, maximize all weekend plans, hit all city landmarks before I get "too old" to explore things like the Statue of Liberty. I have lived in the Financial District for two years and lived a few blocks away from some of the oldest restaurants or bars, dating back to the Revolutionary War or the eighteenth-century. I've never stepped foot in them.

I also know as a perfectionist, there's a part of me that is still teacher and student: BECOME THE BEST CITIZEN POSSIBLE, VOLUNTEER MORE, SHOP AT LOCAL BUSINESSES, VOTE FOR MAYOR. I am on board for all these causes. I want to do all these things. And I will, but sometimes, doing nothing can be a revolt against a world that feels like we may never catch up. In doing nothing, I can join into the local community, notice the trees outside my window, and I can relieve myself of the pressure to do something to prove something. When I do nothing, I contradict the perfectionist idea that I am what I do.

When I did return to Manhattan in January, my roommates and I punctuated our days with walks along the East River. Whether we walked toward Tribeca or toward the Lower East Side, there were a lot of joggers with flat abs and baby strollers and leashed dogs.

The more I went out, the more I recognized trends. In the mornings, there were dancers under a purple-painted bridge who danced in sync with folding fans. Fishermen cast lines over the fenced railings. People played basketball in the afternoons. Some homeless citizens slept on cardboard or yoga mats with a fleece blanket over their head, hiding their faces. I noticed bookstores I never saw before. I watched the ferry move under the bridges, then I learned the bridge names (Brooklyn Bridge, Manhattan Bridge, Williamsburg Bridge).

This is where I found belonging in a city that I wanted to spit me out as my badge of honor. Those walks grounded me in the city as I started to teach myself the landmarks and embed myself into the city, alongside my nameless neighbors, the people who shared enjoying this air or this path or this route as is.

PART 3

"You should be with someone that if you said, 'Let's go kick rocks,' that person would go kick rocks with you."

—MY MOM

CHAPTER 9:

THE POUR

In retrospect, the early spring of the pandemic was not the time to dump money into a skincare routine. Those early months felt like a temporary reprieve from everyday obligations. I had time to exercise during my lunch break. I read two full news articles a day. I had a virtual book club and family Zooms. We didn't know what was ahead, and I batted off the paranoia of an airborne illness by staying indoors and pouring over skincare research.

Before the pandemic, I listened to Luke's sisters talk about charcoal and retinol. My clogged pores sat back, black flags of my ignorance. When did my blackheads conquer my freckles? When did people learn, then implement, these rituals?

The early pandemic felt pleasantly distant. I moved back home for what I imagined would be less than a month's-long stay, and my work at a talent agency dried up. Between formatting actor resumes and watching Showtime, I Googled questions like "Am I at that age when I have to have a steady skincare routine?"

Every article responded, "Are you kidding? Get on it! Your skin will fold like face laundry! Treat those pimples and those wrinkles! How do you have a teenage amount of oil and a horizontal VALLEY running across your head!"

Between jigsaw puzzles, I read. Novels, memoirs, essays, news articles, and newsletters. My inbox sandwiched the *New York Times* next to *Vulture* next to theSkimm. Hard news mixed with instructions to practice self-care with bath bombs, sourdough bread baking, or tie-dying—new hobbies or habits to diversify the days' monotony while infection and mortality rates rose.

A daily newsletter, theSkimm, combines international politics with millennial-isms like "quaranteam." In the pandemic, they made a spin-off newsletter for self-care outlets. "You might have heard, 2020 was a year," the "Press Pause: Best of 2020" newsletter read. "When we headed inside for good, we wanted to create a way for Skimm'rs to Press Pause on the never-ending scary news cycle, the stress, and anxiety of it all. So hi, this newsletter was born."

The first newsletter on April 13, 2020, spotlighted

- a matching sweatshirt set
- virtual games for Zoom happy hours
- cocktail mixology
- seven-minute workouts
- home remedies for root touch-ups
- four-ingredient recipes ("Ideal for dwindling pantries")
- and a plug for a sponsored wellness-habit app subscription

In July, inspired by this wave of "do what you can to allow your brain to survive" self-care content, I had assigned myself some homework—fix your skin. I collected toners, night serums, day serums, moisturizers, and eye wrinkle cream. Though I popped one pimple on my chin into a scar, evidence of an ineffectual combination of creams, I washed my face morning and night.

I stretched the process across thirty minutes, staring in the mirror past my reflection and into nothing, to tell myself I was doing something right. I wanted to assure myself that my skin, in a world turned upside down, could be flawless.

**

I considered feminine hygiene an extracurricular. From high school to college, I measured self-maintenance in ten-minute chunks. A grilled cheese could melt right in seven-or-so minutes, and I could devour the thing in sixty seconds. Showers lasted ten minutes between finished homework and bedtime after 1 a.m. In high school, I slept in my uniform polo and tights to save time. Shaving was a time luxury. In college, my skincare routine revolved around makeup remover wipes.

During these years, I wasn't oblivious to feminine beauty standards. (I mean, duh.) As early as middle school, I ripped perfume ads from beauty magazines and taped them to my wall. I imagined my future success by imagined bathroom cabinets: clean, mirrored, and full of expensive makeup and lotions. My middle school friends and I walked to a local CVS and ogled the beauty aisle until we spent all $50 we earned from a recent babysitting job on eyeshadow and nail polish. I wanted it all, but I didn't have the luxury of time or salary. I was also twelve. Someday, I would have the funds and time to moisturize and/or relax.

During the pandemic, before I was furloughed and after I moved in with my parents, it seemed like all of a sudden,

I had both of those things. Could I just buy the relaxation I hadn't had in seven years?

Because self-care suggests a human re-charge via painting, napping, jogging, and TV watching, self-care is a marketable industry during national crises. Self-care is a catchy idea: put yourself first.

This comes through clearly in the newsletters I subscribed to as they were marketed toward millennial/Gen Z women. theSkimm's aforementioned "Press Pause" newsletter, "The Newsette," and "Girls' Night In" insert sponsored sparkling water or automated pet feeder ads between female-oriented colloquial news, business updates, and lifestyle recommendations.

The staff on "Girls Night In" (GNI) offered pandemic anecdotes that resembled self-care formulas, especially during the pandemic. They redecorated their living rooms via vintage Instagram accounts based on a "sandwich" color palette of pastels. They dedicated a Saturday night to a cookbook and film based in another country's culture to simulate international travel during the lockdowns. They drove to a meadow with their kids. They walked around the block before and after work to simulate a commute in the home workplace.

In Issue #183, GNI founder Alisha Ramos (whose micro wedding landed in *Martha Stewart Weddings* in February 2021, an approval stamp that suggests Alisha is perhaps Martha's millennial counterpart) planned out an entire weekend for readers to survive the August endurance of quarantining:

1. Put away technology and social media until Saturday night.
2. Spend a candlelit Friday night with watercolors or colored pencils.

3. Sip a cup of coffee, have a slow Saturday morning, stroll around the neighborhood, and listen to an audiobook while walking your dog.
4. Do a low-productivity task to cross off your checklist.

"Finally, have a true pamper yourself night. While we all know face masks do not equal self-care, I'm a big proponent of mapping out one night to luxuriate in whatever 'longer' version of your body and face-care routine is. For me, it's doing the works with a double cleanse, face mask, serum, moisturizer, and sheet mask," Ramos says.

This newsletter, for me, is addictively calming. Even the thought of myself replicating these mature routines put me in my fantasy of a clean and over-stuffed adult bathroom. How can these people not only spend so much time relaxing, but also spend so much time...creatively planning how to spend said free time? I eat this stuff up.

I truly believe the GNI writers' recreational discoveries and adventures would fit perfectly in my own routine, even if I never implement them. I trust them to know my self-care better than I do. I would purchase any package that would guarantee me their lifestyle of ethically sourced furniture and interestingly ordinary habits like Friday watercolor painting.

Why can't I just be better at taking care of myself?

**

Self-care has come across as effeminate, a synonym for the powderpuff-fluffy "pampering": essential oils, sheet masks, bath bombs, lavender, tree pose, kale smoothies.

Relief has a price, and it is probably re-sold on a TJ Maxx shelf. A Buzzfeed list from 2017 gives thirty self-care tips that are "So Extra They Just Might Work," which all orient around purchasing something:

- flowers to post on social media
- a candle
- a pajama set
- a maid to clean your apartment
- a massage
- a whole cake
- one movie ticket to sneak into three other showings
- a new sex toy
- a hotel night
- a brand new wardrobe

The distorted focus on needing money to create relaxation echoes the "Treat Yo Self" mantra from *Parks and Recreation*. Aziz Ansari and Retta's characters have an annual day where they treat themselves to clothes, fine leather goods, massages, perfumes, and mimosas.

This fictional excursion is now a catch-phrase for exorbitant spending to placate nationally induced stress, especially after the 2016 presidential election. "The articles began to pop up almost immediately after Nov. 8, speaking to readers in a tone of grave concern, like a dear friend comforting you after a breakup or the death of a loved one," Aisha Harris wrote in 2017 in response to Trump's election. "'Get off social media,' they implored. 'Round up your favorite girlfriends and hit some bars, slam some chasers, and take your rage out on some truly regrettable karaoke.' 'Give yourself a makeover like you're seven years old and at a sleepover.'"

Harris notes how in November 2016, after the presidential election, Google searches for "self-care" doubled. It is hard to imagine self-care as recently mainstream during the pandemic's omnipresent calls to take care of yourself. Originally, the medical term "self-care" originated in reference to elderly or mentally ill patients and the daily tasks they needed to survive (i.e., hygiene and food).

In the 1960s, the civil rights and women's liberation movements used self-care as a protest against racist and patriarchal healthcare institutions. The Black Panther Party created nationwide clinics to address the preventative care and treatment needs of Black men and women; they focused on specialized treatment plans for issues specific to Black communities, such as sickle cell disease and lead poisoning.

"Those programs were established both to make up for the dire lack of adequate social-service programs after the waning of the War on Poverty as well as to provide a coping mechanism against the harassment and surveillance that black people suffered at the hands of the police and the federal government," Harris writes. Likewise, women's liberation groups opened clinics to specifically address women's issues that other, primarily male, doctors had ignored.

For white women, Black people, and other underrepresented demographics, the need to take care of one's physical health fell into each individual's hands. When existing healthcare systems ignored their specific needs or ailments, they took care of their own health. Whether intended or not, self-care was a protest. As Audre Lorde writes in *A Burst of Light*, "Caring for myself is not self-indulgence, it is self-preservation, and that is an act of political warfare."

Self-care, in the wellness lens we know, started with Dan Rather on *60 Minutes* in 1979. He covered a wellness clinic in California. *"Wellness:* Now there's a word you don't hear every day," Rather says to introduce the segment. This wellness wave drew users who sought general betterment, not baseline healthcare. "More people started to discuss the potential to achieve 'positive health' rather than just the absence of illness," Natalia Mehlman Petrzela writes of this trend in *Well+Good*. Being healthy was no longer defined as not being sick. It was defined as making your health *better.* As a perfectionist, all I can think about is how I can be better. Now it was trendy.

"And our multi-billion dollar wellness industry today makes it clear how ingrained these once-fringe ideas have become," Petrzela continues. "Green juice and yoga class, anyone?"

**

"You can be on the best workout regimen and eat all the kale in the world, but if all of these other areas of your life are messed up, how are you going to really meet your goals? How can you really enrich and improve the quality of your life?" Cydney Hamilton told me.

As a pre-med student, Cydney wanted to explore preventative medicine and studied health and wellness. Her interest led her to a public health master's degree at the University of Maryland with a concentration in health equity.

"As I was doing my master's program, the one thing that really interested me was the maternal mortality crisis that was going on—is still going on, honestly," Cydney said. "And one thing that really caught my attention with that, and I just started researching like crazy, is actually the impact of stress, whether that is race-related stress or gender-related stress—those outside factors that weren't diet and weren't exercise were such a root cause for many of the disparities that Black women face."

Within their communities, Black women take care of everyone else. "They hold up the family, hold up the community, and we take on everybody else's stuff. Basically, we don't have an outlet to get that out," Cydney said. Black women through supporting their communities believe that if they are less than the perfect caretaker, they risk the stability they provide their family and community. Cydney believed that she could create a space where Black women could relieve their stress and restore themselves through self-care.

Today, self-care can be self-promotional or marketed through targeted Instagram ads. As a health coach, Cydney doesn't discourage expensive candles or face masks since individuals should cater self-care to their own interests. However, within this same idea, it's important for her clients to realize what works for them individually may not work for everyone. "What I want to do is really help women of color discover what that means for them and providing the space and autonomy for them to choose that for themselves," Cydney said. "Rather than following the trends to say, 'Okay, well, this is what it has to look like.'"

For example, a gua sha rock and jade roller advertised on Instagram might be exactly what one person finds to calm and restore them. Another person, however, might naturally find nature hikes restorative for them, but they turn to an advertised jade roller as their self-care solution. If it works for enough people to become trending, it might be a universal self-care solution. (Spoken from a person who has purchased and thrown out a jade roller when it rusted in the freezer.)

Self-care is not supposed to be a retreat or an escape. "Self-care can be anything," Cydney said. "It can be stretching before bed. It can be taking a nap. It doesn't have to be this super luxurious expensive thing." For Cydney, she takes the time to get her nails done to make sure she is prioritizing herself and allowing time in her schedule for herself.

While Cydney's coaching pushes each individual to focus on themselves holistically—to ask themselves why they want to lose ten pounds instead of giving them a cut-and-dry nutrition and exercise plan to lose weight—she believes in the "pour" philosophy. If each person is a cup, they must find a way to refill and restore themselves in order to pour any energy or effort toward the people they love and support. With Her World Wellness, Cydney pours herself into making a space separate from the world where Black women can put themselves first. In a world of increasing communal trauma, everyone needs to find a way to restore themselves, to fill themselves to the brim.

**

After 9/11, psychologists expanded the discussion around PTSD to include the first responders as well as witnesses to the plane crashes. The diagnosis reserved for soldiers and first responders with trauma-facing jobs now applied to civilians whose lives changed as a result of an event.

With the ongoing pandemic, everyone's daily lives have changed. CNBC released an article on March 27, 2020, only a few weeks into the United States' shutdown, suggesting that there would be long-term emotional trauma from the pandemic. The article suggests the trauma would surpass the impact of 9/11 or World War II.

Similarly, experts and everyday citizens are debating how the pandemic will linger in the nation's consciousness even after the "return to normal." *Psychiatric Times* announced that PTSD symptoms have already been seen in healthcare workers, people who suffered from a serious COVID-19 illness, and family members or friends of those who suffered or died from a serious case of COVID-19. PTSD symptoms have also been seen in those with occupations that included "extreme exposure to aversive details," such as journalists and hospital workers.

Comparable to the 9/11 study, civilians may have long-term effects from pandemic-era stressors such as social isolation, financial instability, or personal grief of lost opportunities and traditions. As someone who had the privilege to work from home when the workplace became risky, I still inventoried everything I touched outside, and sometimes inside, my home. I used Clorox wipes on produce bags and cereal boxes, and I second-guessed everyone else's whereabouts and exposure. I avoided joining the alcoholic mixology trend on social media because I worried I would fall into a nasty nightly drinking habit. I told myself, with all this time returned from cancelled plans, I wasn't doing enough.

This all could be my internal perfectionist wanting to follow every speculative rule offered by the CDC or news sources but living in a lockdown with the potential to infect myself or others did create a real fear that heightened those perfectionist standards on a life-and-death scale.

This constant trapeze permeated all our activities. The CDC surveyed 5,000 people in August 2020 and discovered almost forty-one percent of people said they had at least one adverse mental or behavioral health problem due to the pandemic, including trauma, substance abuse, anxiety, depression, and suicidal ideation.

"Whether balancing activities of essential work with exposure risk, bearing witness to suffering or loss, or feeling anguish or guilt for not 'doing more' during this time, our society is facing great adversity with potentially devastating consequences," according to Robin Ortiz and Lauren Sinko from the University of Pennsylvania.

After acknowledging the collective yet varied trauma responses to the pandemic, Ortiz and Sinko suggest combining individual and community care.

"Communities can respond by enacting equitable policies to help those most vulnerable to trauma and by treating neighbors with empathy and kindness, given evidence that compassion fosters resilience. Acts of compassion can involve delivering groceries or masks to those more vulnerable, posting motivational signs in windows for essential employees, or disseminating mental health resources and hotline numbers to reach those suffering in silence," Ortiz and Sinko write.

Community care provides a solution to saving the self during traumatic times.

This underlines the origin of self-maintenance. From the Black Panthers and the women's liberation movement to Black Lives Matter protesters in 2020, each person in a movement needs their health to protest and activate their own communities. Building a brick wall does no good if the bricks are crumbling apart.

Yasmine Cheyenne, a wellness coach that focuses on "self-care sans the hashtags and the face masks," gave an analogy of each person's energy being a sugar jar. It elaborates on Cydney's "pour" by focusing on what happens if the cup cannot replenish itself. If the sugar jar gives to every person that asks, there won't be any sugar left for things that matter.

"When you're experiencing collective grief like this, it's really important to go back to the basics. We don't need to set these crazy new goals for ourselves...Joy can look different and feel different especially with collective grief. Making space for joy to just be what it is is really important and healthy for our self-healing journeys."

As discussed in the last chapter, it is easy to imagine that there is a "right" way to live. That may mean being a good citizen or a good neighbor, carving out the best twenty-somethings experience possible. Too many mandates to engage in self-care the "right" way will heighten a perfectionist's natural inclination to believe they have not done enough or need to fix something mentally or physically wrong with them. Engaging in the community can help the perfectionist feel a sense of belonging outside of their desired perception to be "perfect."

With this in mind, self-care is necessary, and engaging in the community gives a sense of purpose and belonging. However, how can we seek to restore ourselves, and our community, without turning it into a never-ending cycle of sought affirmation that compounds the internal strife it seeks to sooth?

**

In a perfectionist culture, our self-care trends lean into self-optimization: how can we wire ourselves to be flawless? how do we escape the stress of a workday after we clock out? how can we feel better?

As a perfectionist, my instinct is to "find out how to best fix yourself" (a rough instinct) and "stop being so damn selfish and figure out how to help others" (a paralyzingly condescending instinct). Self-care has become the best sales pitch. It's impossible to think that one person has tried every new technique. Until they try crystals, then meditating, then a new self-help book, how could they know what is best for them? In a world that is busy and perpetuated with trauma, my instinct to search is the easy one.

My Instagram fills with ads for home-waxing kits and pink razors (I don't know how my data learned that I am indeed very hairy). Or Fabletics leggings. Or Fenty underwear. Or Overtone purple hair dye. A quick click for some new bralettes or eye cream lent me control. Within self-care, specifically in the wake of the BLM protests, I realized my money had a responsibility to support community care by sponsoring small businesses. I saw an Instagram post of a steno-pad list of companies that use prison labor (which in retrospect, I should've fact checked for myself). Now I can't allow myself to buy Neutrogena or Starbucks Frappuccinos from gas stations.

Though my skincare purchases at the beginning of the pandemic have either (a) run out or (b) been stolen from that one night I left my car unlocked in Jersey City, I cannot bring myself to buy replacements. What if I am putting my eye cream money toward a corporation that supports outsourced child labor or human trafficking?

I don't want to say that consumerism is either self-care or community care. What I hope to distinguish here is that the personal improvement industry adapts to their audience. A business model exists around self-care purchases for those too exhausted to choose or discover new ethical brands (i.e., Causebox, FabFitFun). Self-care should be free. Self-restoration should not exist only for those with disposable income. However, if there is an object like a candle that aids in your self-restoration, then we can ask ourselves:

Who makes the candle?

How do they make it?

Is this a local company that the pandemic has financially depleted?

Is this a corporation that poses as progressive without reflecting it in their internal structures?

Is this a BIPOC-owned business?

Is this an LGBTQ-owned business?

Do they use factories overseas or other unethical practices?

Ideally, we would be able to find answers to all these questions—or have the energy to do this much research for a dog collar or diapers. But instead, we turn to Amazon, as it ignores the needs of its unionizing warehouse workers, for convenience. The easy purchase allows us to stop thinking for a second about a simple purchase with potentially complicated consequences.

The Good Place demonstrates the layers of our globalized, capitalistic society. Ted Danson's character discovers humans who qualified for the afterlife's "good place" in 1534 had simpler actions. A kid gave a rose to their grandma and earned positive points toward the good afterlife. In the twenty-first century, someone gave a rose to Grandma, BUT he unknowingly purchased a pesticide-infected rose picked by exploited migrant workers off a sweatshop-made cell phone and therefore earned negative points toward eternal punishment.

The world is complicated, and a single product conveniently purchased can come with entangled consequences on the global market, its workers, and its consumers. It is easy to want to be perfect if we want our self-care to double as community care with conscious consumerism. My own perfectionism paralyzes me from buying anything because of this *Good Place* conundrum; I could buy something from the "wrong" place, or I could search for an answer to how to take care of myself and be exhausted as I push through all the "wrong" options. (Jade rollers gave me trust issues.) I have bought things thinking they would fix me by controlling my image and then found myself back to being unsettled once the items' newness wore off.

Here's what I am trying to say: in 2020, between the pandemic, anti-maskers, anti-vaxxers, the election, the insurrection, isolation, and general devastation, it's been a lot. Everyone needs to take care of themselves, but everyone is fried. When we are emotionally and mentally toasted, it is easy for a company to market that they can take the stress away from the work hours, family care, or mental illness you are experiencing. But they can't.

Your self-care routine should be individualized, so you can get to know yourself, learn your strengths, and find joy in *gestures hands wildly* all of this. Then ideally you can give back to others, which is—despite what a culture run on employee burnout might tell you—maybe what we're here to do.

However, your self-care routine should not be dictated by what you "should" be doing. As a perfectionist, I believed because I heard other people talking about skincare and sought articles telling me what to do with my skincare that this newfound and newly purchased routine would magically restore me. I should be doing this, so I did without thinking about why *I* needed this.

In the summer of 2020, as I've discussed, I lived with my grandma. My job there was supposed to be helping her: unloading the dishwasher, making sure to butter an English muffin for her breakfast, and roasting hot coffee.

That summer, I spent lunches with her talking about her grandmother, who immigrated from Ireland at thirteen and started a laundry business in Scranton. We did crossword puzzles. I made her laugh when I accidentally fell and knocked my elbow on the coffee table, and she checked in on me every hour when I was bedridden with a bacterial infection in the same elbow a few days later. She snuck me a plastic bag of silver spoons and a pink pitcher to take to my apartment in New York so I could carry a little piece of her.

In that summer, as I stared into the mirror to analyze each pore, I forgot to see how we cared for each other.

CHAPTER 10:

THE CREATIVITY, INCORPORATED

———

As a film sales/development intern in LA, I also doubled as the company's unpaid receptionist. Besides screening robocalls and fetching coconut creamer and butter from the local Trader Joe's, I groomed the "info" inbox where strangers sent their scripts to acquire financing or producers.

Legally, I couldn't look at the email body if it contained a script. Sometimes, I would skim it to triple-check that it was something to brush off. Frequently, the senders sounded a little desperate, and a little frustrated about the exclusivity of Hollywood. "Without an agent, no one will read my script" became a common complaint.

One person listed their bio briefly. They listed their education under Martin Scorsese and Judd Apatow via Masterclass as their primary experience.

I opened the Word document with our copy-paste rejection: "Thank you so much for considering us. Unfortunately, we cannot accept unsolicited submissions, but we wish you the best of luck." I sent it off, quietly thrilled to consider myself distinct from them, the ones on the outside.

Though I was a student, my short time in LA jaded me. The hope I carried for myself, that I believed I was different with compounding potential, reflected in all the comedy shows, short films, web series, and bad, bad, BAD scripts I read. All of us thought we could be "the one," no matter how much the chase felt like running in place.

Today, there are endless reference guides for any creative pursuit from knitting to screenwriting. To not only study all these reference materials but implement them in practice is a full-time job in and of itself. In order to break through the mold (like Adam's ambition reflected in Chapter 2), my work would have to be the funniest, the sharpest, or the most incisive. In short (say it with me), the work had to be perfect.

How could these strangers imagine that a Masterclass subscription would change anything for them?

**

"Imagine how cool it would be if we could go back in time and take classes from the greats—from Plato, from Maya Angelou, from Gandhi, from the Wright Brothers, from Einstein," David Rogier said. "Even if half of what they said was wrong, how much would we have improved as humanity to take what they have learned and be able to build off that?"

Rogier, the CEO of the online education platform Masterclass, expands his company's scope on a monthly basis. As of my writing this, the classes available include:

- RuPaul: Self-Expression and Authenticity
- Dr. Jane Goodall: Conservation

- Neil DeGrasse Tyson: Scientific Thinking and Communication
- Wayne Gretzky: The Athlete's Mindset
- Tan France: Style for Everyone
- Timbaland: Producing and Beat Making
- Serena Williams: Tennis
- Penn & Teller: The Art of Magic
- Bobbi Brown: Makeup and Beauty

The platform that started with Rogier's idea and courses from Serena Williams and James Patterson has become a cultural hinge. As one veteran Hollywood agent told Rogier, Masterclass has become "the most exclusive club in the world."

While the categories range from the scientific to the artistic, Masterclass primarily focuses on arts and entertainment. From filmmakers like Ken Burns to Spike Lee to Judd Apatow, to actors like Natalie Portman and Helen Mirren, the "arts and entertainment category" hosts fifty-eight available classes to date. Comparatively, there are only ten classes for "sports and gaming" and four for "science and tech."

This unprecedented access to "creative" and previously inaccessible trade information has opened the floodgates. In my (again, probably too jaded, potentially jealous) view, everyone has a creative side hustle, be it a podcast, film short, wedding photography, or a funny TikTok. In our knowledge-based economy, our brains and brands make our money, and we can craft creative projects from our phones. When I catch someone on my Instagram posting clips of their homemade music video or comedy sketches, it grates me. *Why do they all think they have the potential to be the one who breaks out from the anonymous pack?*

With these resources, either via Masterclass or peer examples, the social multiplier effect kicks in. Precious information becomes the baseline. In Duckworth's *Grit*, she explains how James Flynn, who discovered "the Flynn effect" in rising IQ trends over generations, described that TV increased basketball skills. When kids could watch professionals any night from home, they could teach themselves the tricks. When one kid on the blacktop incorporates trick dribbles or the fake-outs that they've seen in the NBA from TV, then the kids they play with also start to incorporate those moves. Everyone gets better, and the next generation of NBA players drafts from this group whose baseline performance mirrors current NBA players.

Today, especially with the pandemic's acceleration of online events, an aspiring anything could find TED Talks, question-and-answer panels, early drafts, revision theories, and communities online. Compare this to Hemingway and Fitzgerald, who had each other and their experiences. They didn't have reference books explaining how to craft a plot.

The quote from the villain in *The Incredibles* slid under my psyche at a young age and haunts me as everyone around me posts their self-released passion projects, their announcements as someone special: "And when everyone's super, no one will be."

To me, Masterclass added to the acceleration of this epidemic pre-pandemic, this stubborn belief that each of us could be special—special meaning famous, newsworthy, critical darlings and audience favorites. *With all this information, are any of us that special? We can't all be pursuing art and not making any money. Someone has got to get into a corporate job.*

I scoffed. None of us were that special.

But if someone was, I wanted it to be me.

**

My internship at Upright Citizens Brigade's then-existing
television development department required I go to theater
shows almost every night and write a brief on the sketches
and acts. I saw five to eight shows a week, sometimes watching consecutive shows and getting out of the theater at midnight. I soon memorized all the recurring performers' names
and formed comedy crushes from the audience on performers who would move on to *Saturday Night Live*—or would
eventually settle to teach improv comedy at the same theater
that made them cultish favorites among UCB students.

The Upright Citizens Brigade theaters (or UCB) in Man-
hattan and Los Angeles have hosted comedians like Donald
Glover and Aziz Ansari in their early stages and instructed
famous comedians like Bobby Moynihan (*Saturday Night
Live*), Ben Schwartz and Thomas Middleditch (*Middleditch &
Schwartz*), and Abbi Jacobsen and Ilana Glazer (*Broad City*).

Amy Poehler, Matt Besser, Matt Walsh, and Ian Roberts,
known as the UCB Four, founded the theater, which started
as the improv troupe "The Upright Citizens Brigade" before
its first theater opened in 1999. The founding four dressed
in black suits, splattered fake blood in the theater, and were
arrested during street performances. They were an acquired
taste like sand on your tongue, and they attracted comedy
oddballs. People dropped their $25 class deposits in a box in
the basement of the Chelsea theater, which were tracked on
Ian Roberts's fridge.

By 2011, fifteen years after the theater's founding, the theater expanded from a former strip club to a bicoastal corporation with a touring theater group and 8,000 students
taking classes. "For the next twenty, thirty, forty years in

this country, the comedy that we will be purchasing as consumers will have some UCB on it," Andy Richter told *New York Magazine.*

By 2018, when I was in the lobby, students spent money at UCB not to be arrested during street performances but to be discovered like previous alumni. The cost reached $450 per class with a four-level pass-fail system. It costs nearly $500 for improv regimen in an art of making it up as you go, though it originated with the founders who risked reputation and record to do something new in an anti-corporate satire.

I felt superior as someone on the inside of the theater who could watch shows and write a report saying which comedians and premises I thought were funny. I worked in the theater lobby—a bright room with a bookshelf of comedy reference books, leather couches, and a friendly receptionist. Every day, improv and sketch students sat on the couches across from me and my fellow interns to recap improv shows they saw, and they discussed each show like Russian literature.

Let's pretend: "I went to the 'WAM Bat: Magically Delicious!' show, and Julia Moreno—oh my gosh, I *love* her, too— stepped out and pretended to be beef jerky in someone's digestive track. Then Manny Smith pretended to be stomach acid giving her an orientation to the body? And their agreement to the base reality was amazing." Bonus to the students if they used the vocabulary ("base reality," "scene agreement," or "game escalation") from the $25 improv manual that three of the UCB founders wrote and required for class enrollment.

The raunchy theater where performers passed around joints to the audience evolved into an atmosphere of constant and hopeful surveillance. Some students at UCB enroll not because they want to pursue comedy at all costs, in the vein of the UCB Four that found comedic acclaim. They enroll because they want a conveyor-belt-style path to success in comedy.

I would know. I bought three UCB classes, including one that sits as a pending online-class credit due to the NYC theaters and training center being shut down during the pandemic.

As I interned at UCB and befriended my co-interns, three Emerson students mentioned that Emerson had adopted a comedy undergraduate major. Since 2016, Emerson students could major in comedy and take classes such as "Why Did the Chicken?: Fundamentals of Comedic Storytelling," "Writing the Tween Series," and "Advanced Sketch Troupe." Other schools have also adopted similar programs. Columbia College Chicago hosts a "Comedy Writing and Performance" program, and NYU Tisch offers a comedy writing minor.

Luke O'Neil, a former Emerson MFA student, questioned if comedy is something that can be taught to someone who is, put gently, not funny. He wrote about the major as a place to unite with other comedians, but it also provided a sense of security through community in a particularly unstable career as a comedian. "A college education of any kind is no longer the guarantee of gainful employment it once was, and no student today thinks she's graduating into a fixed career path. But a comedy career, more so than most others, is a series of ad hoc improvisations and recoveries from repeated failure. A degree like this seems designed to ensure that when they do end up falling, there is a network in place to help students get back on their feet."

As comedy has become more standardized in both its educational materials and scouting locations, aspiring comedians can justify their decisions in the tumultuous career with an educational track that gives some sense of stability in the vulnerable space of creativity. With all the pressure of stability, metrics, and answers, the vulnerability in creativity is compromised, over-analyzed, and optimized for career outcomes. Despite my own eye-rolling—a major in comedy? really? and can everyone please stop verbally recounting improv scenes and suffocating the comedy from them?—I worried. I also wanted stability in this wild career choice I was making. I had always been a good student, brilliant with direction and authority and classroom competition. If a certification from UCB could mean something or build a network for me, then I would pay $450 all over again. And I did. Two or three times. But some part of me told myself that this was an investment in security—a comedy bond.

**

O'Neil, in his analysis of Emerson's comedy program reviews his own incomplete MFA degree from Emerson, "something that should probably preclude me from rendering judgment on the economic value of any type of degree for eternity." He parallels the comedy program with the discussion around MFA degrees: can someone teach someone how to write?

The Master of Fine Arts degree, an advanced graduate degree to study fiction, memoir, or screenwriting, has spiraled a lot of debate because of how it standardizes a subjective art. While UCB uses the same textbook for the tens of thousands of students that pass through its intellectual doors to standardize the comedy code, the MFA degree is offered at 220 universities and colleges in the United States. However, discussion surrounds the standardization of literary standards, despite the varied faculty and syllabi.

The most prominent critique comes from the workshop model. If you have ever been in a creative writing class, you remember it, and you might remember the anxiety that comes with it. Your classmates print out your story, bleeding with red ink, and place it on their desks as they respond to questions from the teacher to provide commentary and mostly critiques. The writer (you) has to sit silently and take notes to avoid creative fragility from derailing the conversation.

My fifth and final year at Penn State revolved around my Master's in Creative Writing, and I took my acceptance into the program as proof that I was a good enough writer to not need it. My first workshop after Los Angeles was about a girl aspiring to be generally famous and taking comedy classes to achieve that generalized acclaim while her cousin/roommate tags along as her emotional punching bag. I wrote the draft right before I had to submit it for my peers' review. It was rushed, but I felt like I was tapping into whatever frustration I had felt in Los Angeles. At the beginning of the class where my story was workshopped, my stomach flipped over. I wanted to know whether it would be a bloodbath or not, but part of me thought it would be fine. I was more nervous about the uncertainty than anything else.

In fact, I thought maybe they—my peers, my teacher, literary journal editors, a literary agent—would love it. Maybe I'd have so much positive commentary that we would run out of time for negative feedback. Maybe there would be no negative feedback at all!

"So, does anyone have any comments for Chloe?" my professor started. No one said anything. One student who studied theater undergrad raised her hand. "You have the actor union as SAG here, but it's SAG-AFTRA," she said. After that, an avalanche of confusion ran through the fine-tooth comb of mock sincerity. My professor in particular thought my story was stupid. "I don't know why anyone would want to be famous in the first place," she said. She laughed at a place where I wrote the two characters, watching a dog pee on the sidewalk, couldn't pick it up. "How would they pick it up? With a straw?" she laughed.

I said nothing—though I didn't mean it like *that*, I meant that the atmosphere in NYC in summer felt full of evaporating dog piss, couldn't they see that?—because I wasn't supposed to until the end where I could ask questions. By that time, I had no questions. Besides the one question of "Did anyone have anything good at all to say about this?" But I couldn't ask that without looking like an ego maniac. An alternative forbidden question would be "Can I take some time in the bathroom to cry this out before we go into Laura's story?" All I said was thank you, and everyone else moved on.

All this shame for a story more-or-less exploring "the one" epidemic, a privileged pursuit by two white girls whose parents paid rent on their sublet as they completed unpaid internships. There wasn't anything too revolutionary or controversial besides my misuse of the Screen Actors Guild and the dog urine thing. My story was very white in a classroom of mostly white peers and a white teacher. This doesn't include how creative writing programs and this silence-based discussion model invite racism masked as constructive criticism into the classroom.

Junot Díaz wrote in *The New Yorker* article "MFA vs. POC" how his experience in a workshop erased race as a discussion and facilitated microaggressions against students of color. "Simply put: I was a person of color in a workshop whose theory of reality did not include my most fundamental experiences as a person of color—that did not in other words include *me*," Díaz wrote. He estimates over 300 students of color have approached him as a professor to discuss the racism they faced in their MFA programs, from a white student erasing "big words" because he didn't believe that's how Spanish people spoke or another student of color noticing BIPOC appeared in stories only when related to drugs or crime.

My critiques of my story hurt in my perfectionist sense of wanting my first draft to blow everyone away, but I didn't have to face an uphill battle to convince my peers or professors that my point of view outside of white culture deserved to exist on paper.

Despite its flaws, the MFA program has expanded. According to the Association of Writers & Writing Programs, seventy-nine writing programs in 1975 ballooned to 1,841 creative writing programs in 2018. Michael Bourne writes in *Poets & Writers* in response to the pandemic, "graduate school has proved remarkably recession-proof as downturns have sent successive generations of young people back to school seeking more qualifications or a career change."

School has become less about the search for answers; it has become the answer to the stagnancy in adult life. "I worry that what students of the arts are often seeking in higher education is nothing more than proof of their own legitimacy—proof that they are for real as creative people, because their degree says so," Elizabeth Gilbert writes in *Big Magic*.

Perfectionists need concrete results, and we obsess over the results instead of the process. To find acceptance in an MFA program means refining a craft and meeting fellow writers, but there is always the distant hope of publishing the

MFA thesis, finding literary representation, and beating the odds into acclaimed writer-dom. In adulthood, there are no grades to provide bumper rails for how well we do; it is safer to return to the structures of education, the institutional expectations that give clear yes/no answers to progress and affirm, for a second, that you're going the right way.

**

While studying at Stanford, David Rogier worked under Michael Dearing of Harrison Metal. Though Rogier appreciated working with Dearing to invest in other people's ideas, he wanted to have his own ideas. Dearing told him to write a proposal, Rogier did, and boom—a check for nearly half a million dollars to invest in whatever company Rogier decided to conceive.

"I mean, holy shit, you think it's really awesome, it sounds really awesome," Rogier said at a 2019 This Week In Startups Fireside Panel. "It is terrifying because it's a once in a lifetime chance I'm never going to get again. It's tons of pressure to come up with a good idea, and I can't complain about it to anyone." Even his therapist, in Rogier's words, said, "I'm sure the stress is real but fucking deal with it."

Without any guidelines besides the extreme amounts of money he received, Rogier flailed under his own ideas. He could maybe do something with supply chains. Maybe something with economics. There were no restrictions, no limits on what he could do. He had complete freedom, and he found that to be suffocating.

Then he met someone—he doesn't even remember who told him—and they gave him one constraint: "Pick something that even if it fails, you're going to be proud of it."

✶✶

Twenty-four-year-old Megan Tan opened *Millennial* by introducing herself as a student who loved school. "I think it's because there's a clear path to achievement with grades, tests, and graduation. Or maybe because it feels like a box that I fit into. It's cozy and comforting."

As a twenty-something with a photojournalism degree and no job offers, she created a seven-page syllabus for herself to make *Millennial*, her podcast crossed with an audio diary of a twenty-something.

She fluctuates between philosophical discoveries and jealousy of her boyfriend's income. She weeps that she thinks she was made for something better, though she is selected as one of ten NPR fellowship finalists. She weeps to her waiter friend about being a waiter. "You kind of want to take your paper and say, 'Look at all the things that I've done! I don't deserve to be here.' Like your get out of jail free card, but it doesn't work."

Hearing Megan, someone who had experienced this postgrad turmoil five years before I did, made me wonder if an entire generation could feel the same way—if we all had this sense of entitlement due to our hard work. I had never heard my own thoughts echoed so clearly in someone else's voice. She hits every check point on her syllabus and can't understand why there aren't equally tangible results in job offers. Near the end of the first season, *The Guardian* spontaneously gave *Millennial* a glowing review. She had a growing fan base. She had sponsors and partnered with Radiotopia to produce her podcast every two weeks. She gained 400,000 monthly listeners.

Yet the podcast was not intended for anyone else to hear. It was not made for results, virality, or a job opportunity. Megan told me she made it with her best friend in mind, since they had frequently communicated internationally through voice memos. "When other people started listening to it, I actually had to have some really intense talking with myself, about doing it for me, and not doing it for people," Megan told me. As *Millennial* expanded into a nationally recognized podcast, Megan achieved her goal of becoming a radio producer for her own podcast, but eventually, she had to step down from it. Though she had growing subscribers and national acclaim, it no longer satisfied her. It no longer was an audio note to her friend across the country.

At that point, she decided to end *Millennial*. We talked about the fear in turning away from the biggest thing that you have built. "I no longer put all of my value in this one thing," Megan said. "I think that's the other part of perfectionism is you feel like these things define you. In this way that is often irrational."

I imagine the short stories or essays I concocted thinking one would land in a literary magazine, get noticed, get shared by strangers on social media. How many of those stories did I actually enjoy writing? How much did I hinge my identity on being someone who "wants to write," and who would I be if I gave that up?

Megan realizes that this twenty-three-year-old version of her that I know through the podcast is not the same person that she was. She doesn't try to measure her own success through a scarcity lens that tells her she either has accomplished something or someone else has. She has found Buddhism and grounds herself in the belief that her purpose in life is to be happy. "Happy is a very strange word to use because a lot of people use it," Megan told me, "but happy is to be so grounded in the value of your own life, just as it is, that anything that's happening around you will not sway your life."

From there, the practice expands into finding ways to bring happiness to other people's lives. "Then we expand with the mission being world peace, because if everyone is transforming themselves in an inner way and transforming... kind of what you're talking about with perfectionism and self-value—if everyone is working on themselves to be happy, then collectively, we'd be good," Megan said.

This blew my mind right up, on the spot. I had never considered that my life didn't have to be building blocks of accomplishments to prove to other people that my life meant something. *Look at this internship! These degrees! My improv shows! Look at this published story, this book! Does this mean anything to you yet?* The question I needed to be asking the whole time was, does any of this matter to me? Would I still be me, even if I never accomplished anything or missed the potential I saw in myself? (What would Dan Pope say?)

"When we put all of our eggs into one basket," Megan paused, "even if the basket drops, you'll still wake up the next day." **

Austin Kleon, author of *Steal Like an Artist,* suggests that all art imitates other art. To learn from the people around you and have increased access to art today is not a bad thing.

I asked him about the trend he saw—both in the easy access to social media that allows each of us to learn and build audiences for any creative projects and that also paralyzes us from acting on it.

"I just think the trend will be people," Austin said. "I just don't think that people will ever go away. I feel personally that when I find a writer I love, it's like making a new friend. I don't want to sound like Holden Caulfield, but when I find a writer I love, it's a lot about hearing a voice and being with a voice. And when I find an artist I love, it's like a hand or set of eyeballs that see things that I want to see."

With a worldview toward adapting (note: not plagiarizing) other people's techniques for your own art, Austin sees the world not as a competition but as a community. This curiosity opens the mind to never stop learning every day, whether that's within an institutionalized curriculum or not.

For example, his sons watch video gamer YouTube streams. Austin's first reaction was, "My kids are just watching this guy and paying for his $3 million house in LA." Then he asked himself—could he steal this? "We were talking about being a perpetual student, being a perpetual learner. What can I learn from these? Obviously, there's some weird thing that's happening with my kids watching these videos. So, what is it? What is happening here?" His own writing includes erasure poetry, drawings, and collages, so he could create a YouTube live stream around making a collage.

"I'm thinking about my sons' futures and I'm like, you keep serving yourself up in a way that, I think the challenge will be not to be a performing monkey," Austin said. "What I'm saying is to do work that makes the world a little bit better. And I'm not judging anyone. I know gaming does wonderful things for people. But for me, at the end of the day, it's like I want them to be privately happy and publicly useful."

Education is something that can create opportunity and community. People can choose to learn whatever their interests might suggest, but education can also be a tool. It can provide insight into ourselves and our plan to give back to a community. The goal doesn't have to be walking away with a diploma to prove you are smart, funny, or creative. It shouldn't be about finding the formula to how everyone else has done it and found success. It should be about learning and listening to yourself within a curriculum or example someone else has crafted from their experience.

True success is unlocking new thoughts for yourself, and perhaps those thoughts can influence other people. That doesn't defeat the barriers to being heard, especially for marginalized voices. It doesn't mean BIPOC writers experiencing racism in workshops or primarily white comedy spaces should just sit and manifest self-actualization until the racism goes away. If anything, it means white people need to spend more time unpacking how they contribute to those spaces (myself included). Whose feelings in my communities have I ignored in my tunnel-vision quest to be "the one," a fragile goal that permitted me to ignore or tear down others in their workshops?

Maybe true success calls for an expectation readjustment. The destination should be fluid if learning creates a spark; I don't need the budget, diplomas for UCB, an MFA, or even Masterclass classes. Unless learning in those places brings me joy, I will learn where I want to go along the way. Maybe that is one of the best things I learned outside of someone else's syllabus.

**

At a Start-up Grind panel, the moderator asked David Rogier what his masterclass on entrepreneurship would be. Though he speaks with a fluid confidence, he paused here.

"Number one would be don't do it," he said.

Rogier experienced his own Masterclass in stress and entrepreneurship by starting his company from scratch. People told him that he would never convince the caliber of experts he wanted to teach a class. What if they agreed and were bad at teaching? With this model, they couldn't launch an A version and evolve it. They had to maintain the promise of the company and not dilute the quality of professors. When you start with Serena Williams and James Patterson, you force yourself to only go up, higher and higher to more prominent experts.

"I lost friends, I put on weight, I slept less, I cried and I don't cry—those are all the costs of starting a company," he said. At every corner, he heard the voices of critics, real or imagined, that told him his idea would fail, even after he booked his first class with Dustin Hoffman.

"I think in our society, a societal norm that we've been trained from a very early age is to get acceptance and praise, if it's from friends, from your parents, from schoolteachers," Rogier said at the Start-up Grind panel. "You get told you get an A; you get told you're doing great. And we almost learn how to not only expect those things, want those things, crave those things, but to actually get good at achieving those things.

"A start-up is the rejection of those norms. A start-up inherently is the belief that I can make a thing happen that other people think is impossible or believe an idea I have is possible and everyone believes is impossible."

The host of the panel smiles. "So do you think instead of opening this with praising you and praising Masterclass I should've said it's not good enough, work harder, twice as many instructors?" she says.

He pauses again and says no, but he has learned to live by his own metrics. "The idea now is when somebody critiques or thinks it isn't going to work, I actually see that as opportunity."

Instead of looking at the models of success that have previously worked, we have to step outside of our own comfort zones, outside of what we know or trust, especially as perfectionists, to find something new. We don't need the A-plus of someone else to drop our baskets, break our eggs, and find a new way.

CHAPTER 11:

THE HAPPY GIRLS

———

"Visi is homey; it's comfortable. People are inviting; the campus is beautiful; and everyone tries to lift you up."

—JOELLA, CLASS OF 2022, VIA GEORGETOWN
VISITATION'S WEBSITE

On the day of my high school graduation, a Visitation teacher pulled me aside on behalf of the institution to threaten me.

"I heard from a few of your classmates that you were behind disrupting the graduation ceremony. If you go through with any of this funny business, I will pull you off the stage, and you will not graduate," the teacher told me and a friend as the rest of our class prepared two straight lines behind us.

The funny business in question involved encouraging class members to lift their hands, gloved to the elbow, and fist punch to the school song, *Cor Jesu.* Complete with droll piano music and Latin lyrics, *Cor Jesu* ended every school assembly or Mass with a clatter of mumbled lyrics and spiked high notes. One particular line had become staccato over the years, the original line *"Vivas et regnes"* sounding like "VIVuh, SET. REN. YAAS." The music director hopped on the mic after one ceremony to say, "Do NOT punch the 'Regnes,' ladies!" So, we had naturally continued to punch the 'Regnes' throughout the school year, and there had been a debate (that I either started or am giving myself too much credit for) around punching the air in mild rebellion at our graduation ceremony, our final *Cor Jesu* as a class.

To Visitation, a playful fist pump during graduation had to be squashed. One final play from the administration let us know that there would always be some risk or consequence to stepping outside the norm.

As the first all-girls Catholic institution in America's thirteen colonies, Georgetown Visitation holds onto tradition as it considers its own place in history. Traditions such as Gold-White or Marshmallow Roast trace back across three generations for some families. The graduation ceremony required that each graduating senior wore the same white dress custom-designed for the class and practiced carrying the rose bouquets in the crook of their right elbow. To break the graduation image that had become associated with the school, though no one but our families would see it, required immediate punishment.

Perhaps it was that paranoia that made me want to do it even more, to say that I could make my own decisions. In the home stretch of my senior year, Visitation had taken away small yet promised privileges. I had been elected to lead school competitions, and I lost all of them publicly in front of parents, faculty, and prospective students. My classmates wound themselves so tightly around college applications that the atmosphere in the Senior Lodge became sticky with jealousy, anxiety, and unshowered bodies. I was boiling for a small, inconsequential "screw you" to Visitation—to at least prove to myself that they had done *something* to me, that this angry stress was not my fault but theirs. Prodding other seniors to join me, it caused a debate about respect and rebellion within our class. People were divided. All of this was in our class's Facebook group, so I knew the class president, or another classmate had pointed me out to the finger-pointing teacher.

And listen again, I get it—I went to a privileged white institution where we had things like "the Senior Lodge." I don't discount that I was fortunate to attend Visitation, that it taught me how to write, that it gave me wonderful teachers and the most thoughtful friends at a cost most couldn't and can't afford. There are pieces of me that love the school still for the people, memories, and education I received.

But also, it was these small mental games that drove me insane. A male administrator made me cry because I had accepted a girl onto a field hockey team, and she said she may have a wedding to attend, and he yelled at me that I hadn't cross-checked everyone's conflicts at try-outs. (P.S.—the student still played in the game because the wedding was a non-conflict.) That same administrator also gushed to one of my friends for going to the University of Michigan, reiterated how smart she was and what a good school Michigan is, and went silent with an "Oh" when I said I was going to Penn State, another Big 10 school.

My math teacher often called out in class that I was the one who struggled at math and mistakenly labeled me as someone they hesitated to put into the accelerated math program. In reality, I had called the academic dean in eighth grade to beg her to take me out of the accelerated program because I hated math, but she said my scores were well above qualifying. I was too embarrassed to correct her because she was the teacher, so I let her think for two years I was too dumb to be in her class.

Teachers assigned hours of homework and projects each night that kept me up until 1 or 2 a.m. When I came into school in my kilted uniform, the dean of students told me that I could unclip the tight button pulling my skirt across "because girls' bodies fluctuate." On our one or two dress-down days a school year, students could not wear leggings or Nike running shorts because they made the small population of male teachers uncomfortable. We sweat through sweatpants or denim in the muggy April humidity of downtown DC. Another male teacher almost sent my friend home from her freshman year dance because her dress was "too tight," and it made him uncomfortable. (This actually still skives me out a little bit eleven years later.)

At the end of the year ceremonies, the entire student body had to attend as the same four or five girls won the academic awards. The top GPAs named as freshman would be the same girls to win everything for the duration of our time at Visitation. I hated myself every year for hoping I might win something, that my all-honors course load and straight A's would mean something.

All I wanted was to mean something to the school as a model of the administration's "happy girl." A Visitation girl, as we learned before enrolling as students ourselves, was happy, well-balanced, well-liked, intelligent, athletic, and artistic. She was everything and more. She was the best at everything, so I strained myself to be everything at once. On the outside, I'm sure I looked it: elected official, cum laude scholar, large friend group, friendly demeanor. I was as close as I could make myself be to the ideal, but I never felt that it was enough.

The other day, as I clocked out of my adult job *seven years* after graduating from Visitation, I felt anxious that I needed to be doing more (folding laundry after doing book revisions while watching a buzzy new TV show). Luke texted me, "This is Visitation in your head, it's not Chloe. You don't need to do anything else."

If I, a poster child of someone who poured myself into Visitation traditions, academics, and extracurriculars until I thought I would bleed our school colors, could be threatened to not stand on stage at graduation for being too "out-there," who really had a chance at being accepted?

In the pictures from that day, on the customary walk from The Green Gate to the field hockey field where the ceremony would take place, I smiled in a sweet farewell to the place that taught me, beyond the lessons on rhetoric and derivatives and the Revolutionary War, how to be a perfectionist.

**

"I've been blown away by this close-knit community and how much the traditions make me feel a part of the Visi family - past and present."

—MARIANNA, CLASS OF 2021, VIA
GEORGETOWN VISITATION'S WEBSITE

"There's a lot you can tell about someone in three hours: Are you confident enough to throw your ideas out there? Are you comfortable enough with yourself to be vulnerable? Is your idea any good? Are the lyrics any good? That is why I lose sleep before a big writing session. Because all of these things come into play, and you'd better be good at them," Maggie Rose, a country singer and Visitation alumna, says about her songwriting sessions.

She underlines the work ethic and discipline she learned in high school as the foundation for her success in Nashville in a Visitation alumnae profile. School traditions like Gold-White helped her translate coordinating her band on the road; balancing tennis practices and meets with schoolwork taught her how to pack her schedule aggressively. Visitation built her "excellent writing, logic, and faith in God and in myself."

This academic push from Visitation is mirrored in other alumnae featured on the Visitation website. "I needed my four years of high school to set me up for guaranteed success. The school offered a unique, yet challenging experience that I knew I would treasure for the rest of my life. (The beautiful and historic campus also sealed the deal)," Katrina Fludd, a current board member and diversity & inclusion specialist at Princeton, from the Visitation Class of 2004 wrote.

Catherine Paul, a Fulbright scholar from the class of 2009, studies for her Master of Social Work at Virginia Commonwealth University, "Even now, a year into my M.S.W., Visitation was my most challenging yet rewarding academic experience."

Current students talk about the academic challenge, the give-and-take dynamic with teachers, the opportunities and Salesian values of honesty, kindness, and cheerful optimism. "It's an environment that makes you want to be your best self, and better yourself," a freshman wrote.

The academic challenge of Visitation is its reputation. In 2010, when I applied as a freshman, its student population mixed enthusiastic legacy students, or students who had family members that previously attended Visitation, and hard workers. Students enrolled to participate in the traditions their moms, aunts, and cousins had participated in (me) or because the academic challenge of new books and at least three hours of homework a night (thirty minutes per subject, as the dean of academics explained in her pitch) was exciting (also me).

An all-girls school can have that hum of excitement, that hybrid of laughter over silly pranks and furrowed brows over books. According to the National Coalition of Girls' Schools, a single-sex atmosphere caters to girls and allows female students to see real-life examples of student officials and mathematicians in their peers.

A common advantage is that alumnae from an all-girls school environment aren't afraid to speak up in their college courses, despite moving into a co-ed classroom. "I was baffled by how few girls were willing to speak in class, and how those who did often apologized for their thoughts/opinions and/or used passive language," former all-girls school alumna Pippa Biddle told *The Atlantic*. The classroom is not a place to present as a docile female partner (smart, but not intelligent or threatening to her male classmates). Biddle admitted that she woke up five minutes before class and didn't bother with makeup; as I've mentioned, I slept in my nylon tights to cut time from my morning routine. In the same spirit of lackadaisical efficiency, I frequently ate cold pizza for breakfast. Some of my friends didn't brush their hair.

Of my eighteen high school friends from the Class of 2014, five enrolled in or are studying to enroll in graduate school to become lawyers and doctors. Three work in the male-dominated industries of finance, technology, and construction.

Five work in entertainment, fashion, digital publishing, or music. Two teach elementary/middle school classrooms. The other six seem to earn good money in marketing or consulting, and they seem to make bank and excel at what they do. (Talk about a creative class, am I right?)

By all standards, we are successful alumnae. As students, we didn't care about romantic relationships more than our report cards. (One of my friends, Hailey, coined the phrase, "Jinx! You owe me a boyfriend!" because none of us knew boys freshman year.) We flipped each other's backpacks inside out as a prank and might make a weird dance competition happen in the common spaces for no reason.

When I asked my friends what they carried from Visitation, they said the following:

- Katie Ward (first year law student): "When I took like an honors class or an AP bio class, I was told literally not to take it because [the academic dean] was like, 'You're not going to do well.'"

- Caroline Laubach (finance): "It's hard to now go to the mindset of focusing on one thing and doing that one thing really well because for so long it was like, have your hands in every as many things as you can and do good enough to get by, but you didn't have enough time to really excel in one thing."

- Nora Dolan (teacher, future law student): "My first semester [of college] I got a straight up D because I took a neuroscience class because I was like, 'I can do all this, I need to prove myself' type thing when no, I shouldn't have taken that class. I didn't want to do anything with neuroscience, and it was just like me feeling like I needed to prove that I could do everything type thing when I should have just chilled out and recognized my strengths."

- Amanda Pierce (construction manager): "I just feel like I thought that literally everyone else was perfect and everyone was perfectly happy. Even all of our friends. I had no idea that my friends went to therapy, too. I had no idea that my friends struggle with this, too, because I even felt that I couldn't open up about that kind of stuff to even my closest friends sometimes because I thought that they were so perfect."

As we unpacked what a Visitation girl looked like, one classmate came to everyone's mind. She was white with silky hair tied with bowed ribbons, carried a color-coordinated planner, was enthusiastic but also quietly tense as if the enthusiasm was manifested stress tweaking. The frail confidence and nerves cooked a fourteen-year-old girl on the brink of a break. The Visitation girl teeters on this edge of bubbly and ambitious, always threatening to fall apart in pursuit of both traits only to push through weeks on the edge of a breakdown. (My one friend endearingly called us "stressed, bubbly elitists.") Complain about your bad grades, bitch about the teachers to your fellow students, but nothing will change. You will stay trapped in this state, quietly picking up more extracurriculars than you can handle.

"I feel like Visitation did make us strong women, but it didn't teach us exactly like what exactly it meant to be a woman," Amanda said.

"It was a cookie cutter version of a woman," Caroline added. "And if you didn't fit the mold, you were out."

We also all knew how it felt to be in a constant state of stress, whether the external factors came from administrators, teachers, or each other. One of my Visitation friends at our college graduation told my parents, "If I'm not stressed, I can't work. That's what Visitation taught me."

**

"I have taught at two other high schools, and I've concluded that there are no girls on earth like Visi girls. They are eager and enthusiastic to learn, they're fun-loving and cheerful, and they're interested in the world around them."

—PEGGY JUDGE HAMILTON, TEACHER AND ALUMNAE (CLASS OF 1985), VIA *GEORGETOWN VISITATION*'S WEBSITE

"Visitation only offered like four or five different AP courses when I was in high school," Mrs. Hamilton said. Though she teaches AP Language and Composition, she now sees students who take all AP-level courses (minus religion, a mandatory but non-scalable course). It would be one thing, she muses, if a student's passion for American history led them to take the AP course; it's another to take a college-level schedule at sixteen with the hope of admission into a "good" college.

Parents approach college counselors angry that their child didn't have any Ivy League schools on their recommended list of universities. Mrs. Hamilton remembers one parent who approached multiple teachers to threaten that her daughter, "Susie Q," needed an A in all her courses in order to play lacrosse at Stanford. Another parent approached Mrs. Hamilton because her daughter, torn between club ice hockey and the school play, was going to fail English. The mother told Mrs. Hamilton, "She doesn't have enough time." Mrs.

Hamilton's next question was why is she signing up for all these things if she doesn't have the time?

"It's like that whole idea like your resume has to be so impressive so you can get into whatever school. But that can't be fun," Mrs. Hamilton says. Instead of teaching students who love English, she finds that more students enroll in her AP Language course to boost their college applications. Students do not think about their individual strengths but seek to be excellent in everything at once.

Though it is easy for students to point the finger at the adult expectations from parents, teachers, or administrators, the young women rarely point to each other, or themselves, as their own prison guard.

School traditions embed competition, both between classes (juniors versus seniors, freshman versus sophomores) or randomly divided halves (the Gold and White teams, assigned randomly or based on familial alumnae's teams). The losses of these competitions provoked extreme responses. When my senior class lost Marshmallow Roast, a skit competition between grades to "roast" the teachers that traditionally the seniors won, we met outside an ice cream shop in Potomac, a neighborhood flanked with million-dollar houses, and jumped on our cars and screamed that our new headmistress was a virgin.

That same year, my best friend and I spearheaded the Gold and White teams in two traditions. This was the position I was elected to lead and failed. There are two annual events—an autumnal field hockey game and a spring basketball game, both including elaborate theme costumes. Everyone treated my best friend like a champion, and I felt that everyone thought I was less capable compared to her. Everyone treated her as a savior, and they still pass down an

Ed Hardy sweatshirt she wore to the line of newly elected Gold Team captains. At the end of the year, we all knew she would win because I lost everything, but she screamed and jumped around on stage. In reality, it's her moment to do whatever she wants, but my embarrassment and anger compounded. For someone who was my best friend, I still hold that unjust bitterness toward her, and we lost touch though we both live in New York.

At any point in my Visitation experience, I carried a low simmering anger. Why couldn't I get this math problem right? Why did the administration have to get on me about having the right type of Sperrys? Why wasn't I as smart as the girls who swept all the academic awards at the end of the year? I could froth at the mouth if I ever let myself get on a rant, but mostly, I told myself these issues were my own and allowed them to boil. I did everything I could to be the "happy girl," and it left me angrier. Why couldn't anyone recognize how hard I had worked? Why couldn't I win anything? The avalanche of extracurriculars, projects, homework, and sports practices kept tumbling, and there was never a moment to acknowledge surviving the past avalanche before drowning and dragging yourself out of the new mountain of work. There was always another avalanche on the horizon— or actively falling toward and on top of you.

Can you put spite a college resume? No, sadly, but my resume still warranted me acceptance into colleges. I wasn't worried about that. They guaranteed people got into college and that after Visitation, college courses would be easier (they were). For me, I was worried that my college acceptance had to prove what Visitation awards had not given me. I wanted to prove myself as witty, intelligent, friendly, funny. As perfect.

Mrs. Hamilton remembered how Visitation hosted visiting schools for Middle States accreditation, a peer-based non-profit that evaluates schools within the network. The teachers saw that Visitation students were allowed to stay in common areas unsupervised and were shocked at the lack of surveillance. But Visitation teaches independence. A student learns to spend her free time studying or goofing off and paying for it later at 2 a.m. "Visitation definitely expects that kids are totally on the ball," Mrs. Hamilton said. Perhaps it's not the teachers who surveil but the students, who watch themselves against their peers. *If everyone else is studying, what are you doing sitting around watching Netflix? You're going to fall behind!*

At Visitation, the valedictorian is both your friend and a threat. I never wanted to take away from the girls who were better, prettier, smarter than I was. Instead, I told myself that I would never be as good as them. Though I graduated as a cum laude scholar (I don't really know what that means, but I got a pin on graduation day after years of hoping to prove I was smart), I never felt like anyone else in my class saw me as someone smart. I held the brightest up the apex I needed to climb toward.

Mrs. Hamilton overhears students brag to each other about four hours versus two hours of sleep a night. When she tells the students that not sleeping is actually not healthy, they bite back, "You don't know what it's like to be us. That's *normal.*"

"It's almost like a martyr complex," Mrs. Hamilton said.

Like most great martyrs we learned about in our non-honors religion class—St. Lucy, Joan of Arc—they are remembered for their suffering.

**

"Visitation is a place where your daughters can truly become who God meant them to be, because it is through the teachings of St. Francis de Sales to 'Be who you are and be that well' that they will face everyday challenges."

— SR. SYLVIE-MARIE, SISTER OF THE VISITATION,

VIA GEORGETOWN VISITATION'S WEBSITE

Education has accelerated our perfectionist society. We grew up in a world of metrics and percentiles since we could hold Ticonderoga pencils and obey a teacher's time signals. We learned that we could compare ourselves for anything on a quantitative level for something as abstract as reading comprehension, and the comparisons weren't limited to our desk mates but the rankings of all students nationwide. This is on an elementary school level before the additional pressure of college admission tests like SATs and ACTs that calculate your intelligence, your future school, and in some twisted sense, your worth. (Don't get me wrong either, this is from someone who loved standardized tests, because I crushed. Not to flex.)

"We're going to set high standards for ourselves because the only way in which we're able to succeed in this society is to achieve high scores, high grades, high performances," Thomas Curran told *NPR*. "The consequences of not doing that is not only do we fall back in school, but that has implications for our college, which has implications for our future market price in the job market." It seems only natural in this market-based mentality of competition and metrics that we want to push ourselves for an objective "best" in the top one percent of anything.

As Mrs. Hamilton said, there were fewer options for students when my parents applied to college. On college tours, my dad was shocked at how many extracurriculars each campus offered—and expected of their applicants. A college degree wasn't ubiquitous. Now, the worth of a college degree has inflated, pushing more and more people toward graduate school in the hopes of setting themselves apart or advancing their career. The expectation of college pushes people into jobs where the loans get higher, and the wages for entry-level positions get lower. We internalize that errors aren't mistakes; they are fractures in our survival.

The first months of my senior year at Visitation were brutal for this reason. A peer asked me what my Vanderbilt application was. I was not applying to Vanderbilt, but she wanted me to know (as someone in most of my AP classes) that she was applying to the prestigious school. Though I wanted to go to a school with a strong communications program, I toured liberal arts colleges like UVA and Boston College because everyone was applying there, despite them not having a program that fit my goals.

Before I chose Penn State, I had a complete melt-down.

"Everyone will think I'm just going to a party school," I wept.

"No one who knows you will think you just went to a college for a party school," my dad said. He listed out all the reasons I knew I liked it: great communications program, close to home, the traditional football college setting, its philanthropic dance marathon. It was big enough that I could do whatever I wanted and never run out of options.

None of these reasons, my reasons, were good enough to save me from other people's judgment.

"Listen," Dad said. "You have to stop trying to be the best at everything. There will always be someone smarter or prettier or funnier in any room. But the smartest person might not be funny. Or the funniest person might not be pretty. But you have the best mix of all of those things. And you have to appreciate that."

The Salesian motto of "Be who you are and be that well" applied to me—though I fit into a shared model of what "being that well" looked like for a Visitation girl (a stressed, bubbly elitist).

When I started at Visitation in 2010, I remember annual tuition being $22,500. The 2020-2021 tuition is $32,600 with an average increase of $1,000 a year in the eleven years since I started. "WE BELIEVE COST SHOULD NOT PREVENT DESERVING YOUNG WOMEN FROM RECEIVING AN EXCEPTIONAL EDUCATION AT VISITATION," the Visitation website reads. "Since our school's inception, the Visitation Sisters have honored this commitment; each year we offer a total of over $2 million in financial aid to one-third of our students." To put $2 million in perspective, Visitation received over $16.7 million in tuition income and fees for fall 2019 according to the 2018-2019 Annual Financial report. (That year also ended in a net loss of one million dollars.)

With Visitation's tuition costs, students largely come from comfortable socioeconomic backgrounds. For some, this cost is worth enrolling in the community that has housed multiple generations of a family. Some grandmothers, mothers, and daughters go to Visitation to participate in the school traditions they all participated in. My last name "Cullen" alone allows a teacher to connect my younger sisters to each other, me, my older cousins, or even my two aunts. For reference, Mrs. Hamilton is one of my favorite teachers, and also one of my dad's best friends from when he went to Gonzaga, Visitation's brother school.

To step into this community without a multigenerational foundation—without teachers who say, "Are you that person's sister?" or administrators who call you by your last name to show solidarity with the familial tribe that forged a path before you—is difficult. My older cousins' examples of Visitation students made me want to attend Visitation and follow in their footsteps. As an eighth grader applying to Visitation, part of me already primed myself for how to be a "happy girl." I washed my yellow uniform polos the summer before starting at Visitation so my shirts would be faded into a near-white yellow, a sign of a hand-me-down shirt from an older sister within Visitation students. I marked myself as someone who wanted to be recognized as "on the inside" before I ever stepped foot into the school. Most other freshman showed up with dark yellow shirts on the first days, and it marked them as doubly new. This financial and social wealth recruits a specific type of Visitation student.

Perfect does not always translate to "the best" but can also translate to normal. Perfectionism is the simultaneous pursuit of the best within the norms given, as we saw in the perfectionism pendulum of fear and burnout. All students have to mask their pain to appear normal and the best, but students who don't fit into the larger picture of a "normal" white, ribbon-wearing and color-coordinated varsity and straight A students are spotted, differentiated, and either ignored or ridiculed.

As each student fell under our own avalanches of pressure-induced expectations from teachers, parents, peers, and ourselves, the Visitation students of color also had mountains of internalized racism in classrooms and common areas holding them back from being considered for the non-existent summit.

In a setting that focuses on one ideal image, anyone who falls out of that poster child image, even aesthetically, is at risk of being seen as different. Think of "the backpacker" described in Chapter 2 who comes in with a different perspective and makes their coworkers double down on norms and traditions. Anyone different can be seen as a threat to stability.

In the summer of 2020, as institutions reckoned with their ingested white supremacy, an Instagram account called "Black at DC Private Schools" listed various microaggressions that students faced within the DC area. The anonymous user had designed the Instagram posts to match a school's colors. Most of the Instagram tiles reflected kelly green, the color of a Visitation kilt.

The few anecdotes range from white girls bragging about how their spray tans made them darker than their Black peers or how white students claimed they wished they were minorities so it would be easier for them to get into college through affirmative action. "As soon as I came to Visitation I was only really welcomed by other students of my own race (African American). The white people, for the most part, already knew each other…I feel that's why so many of the black students end up befriending each other because we all feel ostracized," one post read. This undercurrent of perfection, in ambition and norms, is especially painful for students who cannot be accepted into the mold based on appearances alone.

In 2016, Visitation launched a third-party investigation into its history with slavery. On Visitation's campus, there is a solitary brick cabin by the tennis courts that we jokingly called "the slave cabin," as if the contrast of a tennis court and slave jokes in that sentence doesn't hint to the cultural callous. We didn't question that this label might arise from a real connection to slavery, but the Enslaved People Project Task Force discovered it was. These historians confirmed that the Sisters of the Visitation had owned at least 121 slaves between 1800 and 1862.

Some people may not see how the actions of nuns in 1862 reflects Visitation in the twenty-first century. It is important to understand that in its history, Visitation promoted white people's comfort over human equality. Though the nuns taught their slaves, it established a dynamic that education for Black students was a "gift," an act of a white savior. Micro-aggressions were rampant from white teachers and students toward students of color, and most of these acts happened without the white person realizing or considering how they hurt the Black student or student of color.

Cydney, the founder of Her World Wellness, was one of my Visitation classmates, and at one point during our self-care interview, she said in passing that Visitation did this perfectionist thinking to us. "I think there was a lot of comparison and feeling like I needed to, I'm not gonna say, 'not be myself,' but fit in by doing things that I guess I wouldn't normally do. Like, 'Cydney, you can't be the only person and one of the only Black people who's not fitting in.'" It wasn't until she got to college where there were more Black students that she felt less surveilled at school.

In a culture with a white administration, a primarily white teaching staff, and a predominantly white student body, students of color had to perfect themselves into the "happy girls" to fit into an environment that only saw them as other.

While BIPOC students now makeup roughly thirty percent of each graduating class, Mrs. Hamilton could understand how the lack of acceptance at breaking the mold in a general sense could doubly apply to Black students or students of color. She is a white woman, but she has led the diversity club to provoke hard social conversations among the student body. Her class requires a research paper on either the Vietnam War or mass incarceration in the United States, and her class dynamic is shifting to include more Black students and students of color.

In my time in her class, we had Socratic seminar about censoring or including the n-word in *Huckleberry Finn,* but there was only one Black student in our class. Mrs. Hamilton said before the admissions shift, that was frequently the case. "I'm like, 'That's awful,'" Mrs. Hamilton said. "Why does she have to be the only one in the room? So, I do feel like that's changing a bit. But there isn't a lot of acceptance of being your own person, and if it doesn't really fit that mold, yeah, I definitely think we could do a much better job of that."

Visitation's dean of academics had a reputation for calling all of us "happy girls," as if the more we heard it the more we would believe it. I don't know whether it pulled us further back into our masks or it offered a promise—if you learn to do everything right by us, we promise that you will eventually be happy.

We learned anxiety alongside history, perfectionism alongside geometry. I thought it made us unique and forged us into soldiers of the world. In reality, we slacken our fists, drop them by our sides, and step in line, white dress after white dress.

**

My sister graduated from Visitation this past week. I sat through the ceremony, watched her walk through in her white dress with red roses. They offer a pantsuit alternative to the dress, and a dozen girls wore it with their roses.

The headmistress, the one that my class spitefully called a virgin in her first year at Visitation, gave a commencement speech. After seven years, she's leaving for another school. In her speech, she said that we do not aim for perfection every day since perfection is impossible; however, we do strive for excellence every day in everything we do.

I looked at the girls on the stage who braved Visitation through a virtual school model—all school and no friends would have been dangerous for my mental health my senior year—and they all smiled to each other, excited to move to the next thing. On the final song, alumnae are supposed to stand with the graduating class and sing along. I didn't stand or sing, but I laughed to myself when the class, intentionally or not, lightly punched the "et regnes."

CHAPTER 12:

THE COMMONPLACE CASE OF CHLOE CULLEN

───────

ABSTRACT

This case study outlines the perfectionism listed in patient, Chloe Cullen. She recognizes her perfectionist tendencies in past experiences, yet cannot prevent herself from repeating them in the present moment. This conflict between her reality and expectations creates a disorientation of her perceived reality. She seeks to improve her current state by undergoing close objective scrutiny as a case study subject.

CONTEXT ON CHLOE

Chloe is a twenty-five-year-old white cisgender female. No medical conditions. Deviated septum surgery at fifteen. Heart rate is 120/70. Lung capacity holds at ninety-nine percent. No prescribed medications.

Born December 22, 1995, and grew up in Washington, DC. Oldest of six kids. Attended private Catholic institutions for K-12 education. Graduated cum laude from high school. Went to Penn State. Graduated magna cum laude with a master's and two bachelor's degrees. Now lives in Manhattan, works at a talent agency.

MEDICAL HISTORY OF PERFECTIONISM

Below is a retrospective list of the incidents Chloe associates with her perfectionist tendencies:

Workplace-related
- before job interviews where she scoured the entertainment trades for updated press and information about small companies
- during job interviews where she catered her answers to fit whatever the recruiter might want to hear, resulting in vague answers like "I just really love to work"
- when her agents pulled her aside into the large, empty conference room and said she had to take her lunch break because when she didn't, her work was sloppy; she cried quietly at her desk for one-and-a-half business days

School-related
- before graduate writing workshops she told herself that everyone hated what she wrote and would tell her to her face in the classroom
- when she had a panic attack driving to Visitation because she forgot a spray-paint banner for a school assembly and consequently forgot to pick up the last member of her carpool
- during the college application process when she told herself people would think she was dumb unless she chose an Ivy League college

Socially-related
- when she had a panic attack in eighth grade as her dad drove her to a stranger's house to get ready for a dance because she worried that everyone was talking about her as the weird, uncool girl, and that they already were laughing at her
- during any and all conversations where she kept her thoughts to herself to avoid "making a fuss"
- whenever she got frustrated at a sibling or roommate for not unloading the dishwasher, before she also proceeded to ignore the steaming, clean plates and the sink full of used cutlery
- when she told her Significant Other (S.O.) that she felt he didn't appreciate her enough, or didn't show it, or at least she couldn't see it in the gestures he constantly made
- when she snapped at her brother for being too loud, too controversial, too much for the dinner table

Image-related
- every time she looks at her stomach in a mirror
- every time she looks at her cellulite in a mirror
- every time she looks at her jaw in a mirror and remembers that she doesn't have a jawline
- every time she sees a peer accomplish something via Instagram or LinkedIn and feels a pang of jealousy and nerves, as if that position or accomplishment could've been hers but now it's occupied
- every day since January 2018 in Los Angeles when she told herself she had to write every day to be a writer that she does not write anything and considers herself a failure

Patient presents with anxiety symptoms. Her days are heavy with negative thoughts, like wearing damp clothes. She writes yet is stressed about the inconsistent habit. She starts virtual therapy. Therapist suggests that the patient's anxiety wouldn't exist if she just wrote instead of feeling anxious about it. The patient takes the suggestion and becomes more anxious. The therapist assigns homework tasks of to-do lists. The patient does not do the homework despite her repeated love of lists because the tightness of stress doesn't go away, and the to-do list is one more thing on her generalized to-do list.

Patient switches therapists.

Patient has recently moved back to New York apartment. She lived at her parents' house from March to June, then lived with her grandmother from June to Labor Day. Her significant other recently moved to Manhattan. She has visited him two or three times in this five-month span due to COVID exposure risks. Before this, their relationship was long-distance from December 2017 to October 2019. She talks about "the honeymoon period" and reflects nostalgically about their first months—the Christmas café, the FaceTimes across time zones. The patient and her S.O. met before her Hollywood internship program. In the two weeks before she left for LA, they met each other's friends and families. They spent five days straight together. They celebrated New Years. She floated. She had never felt that way, itching to see someone and be comfortable with them.

On their last day together before she left, they sat in his car parked under the Thirtieth Street bridge to wait for her bus. He bought her ticket, the first seat on the double decker. It could feel like flying, he thought. Before they were bantering and joking. As they turned toward the bus stop, she summarized Casablanca for him and said they would always have Paris, this moment, this feeling, in whatever happened to them. He said that he believed in the butterfly effect. When she got out of his car to board the bus, he looked at her and cursed like someone punched him in the ribs and kissed her one last time.

Patient worries about moving in together and losing her independence in a new setting. She never volunteers her thoughts on restaurant selections. She never volunteers TV shows and suggests whatever she thinks he wants to watch. She starts to resent that he doesn't push more. She brings her laptop to his apartment and works from his bed most weekdays. She plays with his cats. She kills time.

She tells her S.O. that she wants to write, and he tells her that he will give her whatever privacy, room, and time to do so. Still, she doesn't write. It brings her an everyday itchiness of determining when she will write until the act of writing itself, in the abstract, does not seem like a relief but a fear. She doesn't write. She tells herself that something is wrong with her: her endurance, her discipline. She conflates her negative relationship with writing with her affirmation of her S.O., how easily she chooses to do nothing with him. She could waste all her days like this. She tongues the phrase "waste all her days" like a marble, and the tightness is there, and she wonders if the problem isn't her but him.

DECEMBER 2020

Patient returns home for the holidays and cannot write a word. She spends days watching movies or buying gifts with her siblings. She sits on the couch and texts other people to make them tell her it is okay that she's not writing. Every family moment comes with a sharp internal dialogue. She hates herself because she can't write (and what kind of issue is that really? if she had inky fingers, this wouldn't be an issue). She hates herself for thinking her writing is more important than being with her family. She plants herself equally in both realms, the living room and the expanding debate in her brain, until they stretch her apart, like two trains in opposite directions. Each time her siblings put on a movie to watch with her, she blames them for how she feels. The smudge of wrongness must fall to someone else to soothe the patient's mind, even if it doesn't work to alleviate her anxiety about what she "should" be doing.

Patient turns twenty-five.

Patient volunteers to go to S.O.'s family the day after Christmas. She cries during the car ride to Philadelphia. Every time she leaves home, she tells herself that she has hurt her family by leaving. *What could be so important to abandon your family on December 26?* Her family never says this and never would. The patient assumes this pain because it makes it harder to leave. Sometimes, she thinks she only feels love in imagined absence, the hypothetical void of disappointing someone. Their silhouettes do not reciprocate affection. The patient holds onto the shadowed figures of the people she loves to remember they can always leave.

She drops off her S.O. to play cards with his friends and wanders the grocery store to buy wine and ankle socks. She spends too long thinking about her choices and goes for two $15 bottles to bring to his family.

JANUARY 2021

The patient and her S.O.'s entire family test positive for COVID over the holidays. The patient quarantines with her S.O. and her S.O.'s mother. His mother's breathing worsens.

The patient calls her dad, a doctor, and feels guilty that she is solving someone else's family health issues to his face right after leaving them. When her S.O.'s mother goes to the hospital, she rides in the backseat while her S.O. drives. She listens to them talk about the routes to familiar restaurants from his childhood. Her S.O. talks about the past to soothe his mom, and she does seem calmer. Her S.O. gets his mom to the hospital entrance, a tent tunnel, and his mom seems less scared.

January revolves around his mother's days in the hospital and their days in her empty house. The patient had picked up an unpaid internship to fill her employment time. She feels guilty about telling her boss she has COVID and can't work. She feels guilty that she can't work on her book. Her book editor tells her that she should rest to avoid inflicting worse symptoms. The patient wants to get work done, but not because she wants to work. She wants the work and the tightness that comes with it to fall behind her. She doesn't want to do anything.

Her S.O. calls out of work. Both of them sit on the couch and watch all forty hours of *Better Call Saul* in five days. They do nothing together.

One night, the patient measures her heartbeat and lung capacity with the Amazon-ordered pulse oximeter. When her S.O. clamps it to his finger, he teases her and hides his results. She chases him and runs back into her own childhood, chasing her siblings and looping through each room on the first floor as they screamed. The adrenaline kicks. She laughs. So does he. She forgets to worry about their breathing, whether her or his chest is heavier with latent lung symptoms. They stand on opposite sides of his mother's kitchen table, panting and laughing. She finds herself relieved to be the chaser. The one who decides when he stops or goes. The one who sets the terms. He calls a timeout, and they both stand there, breathless and smiling in the simplicity of a chase.

FEBRUARY 2021

People talk conversationally about the patient's book to tell her they're proud of her. She hasn't written a thing between Thanksgiving and the end of January. Her motivation is diluted. On a bus ride home after the funeral of her friend's mother, she cries out a bus window. She listens to sad-girl albums and realizes people might love her. The book creates a spell. People become more solid. *It's always been about the people*, she thinks.

In therapy, the new therapist always asks how she feels about moving in with her S.O. that week. The patient diagnoses herself with a fear of commitment. She never had a fear of commitment before; she has been in one long-term relationship or another since she was sixteen. The patient fears domesticity, adulthood, boredom.

She thinks but does not say: *One day, I will wake up and be a suburban mom in an apron cutting flower stems and my life will be normal and it will be worth nothing.*

She imagines there has to be something more. She imagines, every day, that the door she wants open closes a little bit every day, no matter how quickly she runs to catch it with the toe of her shoe. She doesn't even know where the door is. She doesn't know what the door leads to. The act of catching it, however, suggests a freedom, and wouldn't that be enough?

The S.O. takes a ski trip to a different coast. The patient debates dying her hair purple as a living moral to her book. *The remedy is to stop caring what people think of you, so you wear what you want in spite of other people.* She tells herself this will be the weekend she dyes her hair. It isn't. This is the weekend of the long car ride.

She and her roommates get into a Lyft to go to a friend's apartment. She thinks about the book and the conclusion she thinks she has discovered about life (*it's about the people, but who cares what people think of you*).

The patient sweats. She watches the city landscape, black on a navy sky. *You think you have this all figured out, like you're above everyone else with this new secret of life, but you're a hypocrite. You're hiding from yourself. You stifle yourself every day. Purple hair won't change that.*

The patient's perfectionism called out something that the patient otherwise would ignore. *You're a hypocrite. You are pretending that you can keep being the way you are so people will like you. You think you've solved it, but you're really a fake. You want to ignore the piece of you that might jeopardize your normalcy.*

The patient is confused why now, why ever. *Just shut up.* Without a word on the radio or from her friends, her thoughts rage against each other. *You shut up. You're a hypocrite and a scam. You like girls. You've ignored it all these years.*

She doesn't know why then. She does know that something about this thought has been shifting inside her, a wasp flying into the walls of a glass jar. She doesn't know what else it could mean. Does she have to fix it or solve it or revise it?

They reach her friend's apartment. The patient gets out of the car. Her roommates were there the whole time, silent in their own thoughts. She says she had too much time to think in that Lyft, and then she dismisses it all. She talks about her friend's water speakers and eats Chick-fil-A. In these conversations, she talks to no one but herself. *You like girls, you like girls.*

She goes home and writes in her journal. She goes on for ten pages, listing the questions she has about who she is. To see it written down makes her feel that some of these thoughts are real. The bisexuality. The orgasm disorder self-diagnosis in its earliest articulated form. It also makes her feel incredibly lonely because she doesn't know who she can tell this to. She is scared to tell her S.O. She is scared this feels too big, too wide for them to figure out. *This will create a ripple effect. This will change everything.* She turns to her therapist, sends pictures of the pages because the therapist feels like the only relationship in a vacuum, someone who won't have opinions on anyone but her.

That week, she speaks to her therapist in an emergency session. Her therapist suggests that this makes sense. The orgasm disorder might mean she is only attracted to women. It might mean she breaks up with her S.O. to explore. The patient breaks into tears. *I feel like I'm going to blow my life up,* she repeats. The therapist tells her that she can't love anyone if she can't love and accept herself. Her S.O. deserves better than this, she thinks.

The session ends. The patient is in the "work lounge" of her apartment building with her head down on a table while strangers, her neighbors, work in other enclosed office spaces. She still has told no one in her life about this thing, this internal conversation. The patient sobs in the shower long enough that her roommate quietly asks if everything's okay. The patient says nothing. *I wish that I could take this away, I wish I didn't have it.* She sets about fixing herself back into the partner she was—or the partner she thought she was, now that she sees herself as different, as a flight risk. She Googles "bisexual in a straight relationship" and reads Reddit threads of couples who tried and couples who broke up.

After a few days of crying in their small apartment, the patient comes out to her roommates. She tells them about the orgasm disorder, about how she physically cannot love herself. They treat her S.O.'s love as fact. *He loves you so much. He will be understanding.* There must be something wrong with the patient. He loves her so much. He will be understanding. Would she give him the same love? Is there something doubly wrong with her that her love isn't as absolute? That she has these questions that might pull her away? *Do you even love him? Why would you do this to him? Is this why you're scared of commitment? Is this why you worry about the butterflies?*

One of her roommates turns to her and suggests that if she can't do this—the self-love—on her own, then that is a separate issue that sleeping with someone else won't fix.

In one of their November fights, she kept telling her S.O. the honeymoon phase was over. She asked if the butterflies were gone. He said they had been replaced with something better. The patient wanted a recipe or diagnosis for her feelings three years into a relationship. She could not trust her own feelings. She could not know herself outside of being perfect.

Maybe another person would fix it. Maybe she's not enough for her S.O. Maybe she had held onto him to make herself feel better and held him captive to love her. She oscillates between thoughts that she's selfish, selfish, selfish—no matter what she does, she is going to hurt someone.

The patient lies horizontally in bed and can't stand up. She cancels a dinner plan. She can't look at her Bluetooth frame that carousels pictures of the people she loves—her siblings, her high school friends, her cousins—who don't know who she is.

Her roommates take her on walks. One roommate puts an arm around her while they watch the sun set over the Brooklyn Bridge and says, "It's going to be okay." The patient doesn't know if she can trust that, that okay can be enough. This roommate puts the patient in touch with one of her college roommates who came out after a three-year relationship with a guy. When you text your roommate's former roommate, the former roommate says she falls more in love with her partner every day. She couldn't spend a minute without her. They met on a dating app during the pandemic, and now they live together with multiple animals.

"We were like that," the patient says. She thinks of her S.O. He texts her updates about how quickly he skis down the mountains in Idaho. She sends pictures of his cat that she watches at her apartment. *We were like that.* She doesn't know if they're different now. She doesn't know whether they're the same or different than this former roommate's same-sex relationship.

The former roommate talks about her ex-boyfriend of three years and how they were comfortable but could never talk about periods or be comfortable. ("We can talk about periods," the patient says. The former roommate doesn't give her the affirmation, the gold star that discussions around menstrual cycles were all the former roommate was missing in her heterosexual relationship.) They were fine, but never anything exceptional. *How do you know if you're in the exceptional range?* The patient wonders if dating a woman is a utopia free of the patriarchal norms of a heterosexual relationship. *Who would wear the apron? Is it like living with your roommates, but romantically?* She has no idea. She can't get up from bed.

Her S.O. calls her from an airport. The overhead speaker calls for groups to wait or board. The conversation is dry. The patient gives him nothing but empty air and clipped responses. She thinks about the honeymoon times. They always called each other from their airport gates. He always made her laugh.

This is different. We are different.

Both voices sound exhausted as he runs through an outline of his skiing statistics. He has had a hard year. He needs to not be worried about someone else during this one trip. The patient breaks her own promise and tells him that she has realized something. She tells him she's bisexual. On the Reddit threads, some users wrote their partner nodded then went back to his meal when he found out. Her S.O. cries in the airport. He is so proud of the patient, but he asks—and hates himself for asking—if this jeopardizes the forever they had known and felt and discussed with each other since day one.

The patient, the answer-seeker, doesn't give him a definitive answer because she doesn't know.

MARCH 2021

When her S.O. returns, the patient meets him at a sports bar painted in blue light. Over a waxed wood table and bouncy chicken sandwiches, her S.O. says he knows he really loves her, because even if he has to lose her—even if she dates another woman—he wants her to be happy more than he wants to protect himself.

The patient tries not to cry, tries to explain that it might also be that she's scared of a heteronormative lifestyle. The aprons. The chicken parm. The scarcity. She has it figured out. She has answers. Internally, she still compares her response to his. *Why did his answer come across as more genuine? Is there still something wrong with me? Do I deserve him?*

A few weeks pass, then a month. They don't talk about it besides in abstract conversations about jealousy, about what "exploring this" might mean. Neither of them knows. She avoids the conversation, and that seems to work. She and he lean into each other. She worries that he has put a guard up to prioritize her. *Whatever makes you happy.* He tells her that this doesn't change anything for him, she doesn't have to worry, but she only knows how to worry. She doesn't know how to make herself happy. She goes to his apartment and keeps doing nothing with him. It's what makes her calmest— nothing, next to him. She finds relief in his consistency, then starts to loop on herself. *You are the inconsistent one. You are using him. You are a terrible partner. You are a terrible person.*

Some days, she can ignore her thoughts and wrap her arms around his torso to buoy herself to something or someone real.

At the end of March, she wakes up feeling anxious and naked. She tells her S.O. that she feels disgusting—heavy, guilty—and he says that she needs to explore this at her own pace. He says, "You probably need to explore this, whether it's in a month or in a year. And whenever you're ready, we will work through that together." This understanding spirals her. Is this what she wants? Does she want to date other people? Or does she just worry that there's some alternate life of hers that could be better, where she makes more money and is more creative and is happy with herself?

That weekend, she feels the butterflies again. Someone asks what her first impression of her S.O. was. She says showered and clean, and he smiles. When he looks at her then, she feels like it is that first time, seeing him walk down a staircase in his college house. The next night, when she walks up a staircase to their friend's apartment, the patient bumps into him walking down the stairs for a bodega mission. He is so excited to see her, and she is so happy to see him, that they sit on the stairs thigh to thigh. He whispers that he's so happy to see her.

To each happy moment, her mind has a counter. *You're only happy to see him because he's your security blanket. You're only happy being around him because it's safe and you are going to corner yourself into a life of inauthenticity. You're holding onto heteronormativity because you're homophobic. You're wasting his time. You can't feel love. You don't deserve the love he gives you.*

From that Sunday to the following Friday, she entered into a five-day sweat, a starvation of stomach and sanity, as she stared at her computer and sent audition emails to child actors on auto-pilot.

SYMPTOMS OF THE FIVE-DAY SWEAT

When absorbed with an extended perfectionist stint, the patient presented with the below symptoms:
- Blood rush to her ears whenever she thought about something she didn't want to think about
- Loss of appetite for five days
- Loss of weight due to loss of appetite
- Sporadic tears quiet enough to hide from her roommates
- Huge gasping sobs and rants to her roommates
  Besides Chloe's physical symptoms, she also experienced:
- extreme and battering self-doubt
- relentless self-interrogations on any argument she presented to herself

- disconnect between her thoughts and the present that left her brain "floaty"
- refusal of other's opinions and input
- stubbornness to fixing herself
- guilt in crying to her roommates about her problems

APRIL 2021

The five-day sweat ends, and the patient has no answers. She is worried she's doing something wrong. She is worried that she is at a fork in the road and has to make a choice for forever.

The patient came out to her parents in the backseat of an Uber as they drove home from a restaurant. *How do you know if you're with the right person? Are there metrics for how someone should feel three years into a relationship? What if I have to date a woman for three years to know that I want to be with him? What if I date a woman and I end up with the same doubts as I'm having now?*

Her mom told her, "It's not that deep. You need to cut yourself some slack."

The patient wanted answers to prove that she was on the path to living the most optimized future. She wanted a significant other who told her how to love. She wanted parents or roommates to tell her what to do with her life. She didn't want to be accountable for her own decisions, and she didn't trust that she could make decisions for herself.

At one point, she watched a TikTok of her bi friend and her bi friend's girlfriend. They painted a circle on the wall of her friend's bedroom. *That is what that female relationship must be like, she thought. Trips to the paint store. Arts and crafts. Doing anything together.* The patient had never wanted to paint an apartment wall, but she wondered if she had any friends who would paint one with her if she ever wanted to.

The patient never realized that she could do these things by herself. If she wanted to paint, she could paint. If she wanted to take photos, she could take photos. She did not need a partner to unlock her creativity, to tell her she was doing something right.

The patient and her S.O. traveled to Nashville for a belated twenty-fifth birthday celebration. The travel agency sent a full itinerary with suggestions for local restaurants and landmarks. The two of them took some suggestions and ignored most. The patient wore blue eyeliner and butterfly earrings. They wandered the Johnny Cash Museum and ordered grilled cheeses. They lay in a hotel bed and watched the first season of *The Sopranos* instead of visiting the honky-tonks on Broadway. Someone else's travel arrangements would always serve as a guideline. There would also be another restaurant or landmark to run to. A place to see for the sake of seeing it before the trip ended.

None of those travel arrangements would brag about the luxury of falling asleep, full of linguine and meatballs in a barbeque town, while the restaurant that was two blocks away had guitar blaring from its speakers.

For the first time, the patient realized she could decide, and she decided that this was enough.

AFTERWORD

The patient has given up on seeing life as a race. She doesn't know who she was competing against, and if they lap her, then she will never know how their success deprived her of a potential accomplishment. When she worries about the scarcity mentality, she thinks of bookstores and their colorful shelves of thousands of people's thoughts, side by side with someone writing the same subject slightly differently. She would rather look back on her life and remember the little moments—sweatshirt days on a boardwalk mini golf course, a stubbed toe at her grandma's place, or the near weightlessness experienced on a swing set—instead of burning through all her days to cash them in on one big career goal.

She has had other fevers of identity anxiety since the April Nashville trip. Her friend Vas showed her a list of common cognitive distortions—all-or-nothing thinking, "should" statements, magnification or minimization—that the patient recognizes. *These are all perfectionism. I do all of these.* She has reviewed dialectical behavioral therapy and mindfulness. She accepts that she only has this moment, the right now, and twisting her future and past into a knot will only steal those moments. Sometimes, when she believes her thoughts want to spiral her into another reality, she is learning to ground herself and stay still.

It is what it is, she tells herself.

One day at a time, she tells herself.

You are where you need to be right now, she tells herself.

She doesn't have to be or do or decide anything that will make someone else happy. She realizes she can love herself. She realizes that she can give herself permission to enjoy the relationship she's built. She realizes sometimes that she does deserve this love, and sometimes, she surprises herself by recognizing when she loves him back, just as much, just enough.

The patient got a job, a job that she could only dream would be her first job when she graduated. She realizes that sometimes dreams and goals become reality, then they're just there.

She still hasn't painted designs on her walls or picked up an artsy hobby, but she no longer blames her S.O. for making her hobbies his priority. *And how are you crazy?* She recognizes these high expectations are part of her crazy. Part of her wants to set time aside to take herself on a date, to figure out who the patient is or what she wants. She might write dumb poems, paint with watercolors, bake, learn how to garden, study her own butterflies. She might read.

Whatever she chooses, there is a book on a shelf, sitting among a dozen other books on knitting or fiction-writing or gardening. It will belong entirely to the person who wrote it and the person who holds it. Together, they'll grow their shelves and their minds. They will stop searching for the answers to perfect themselves. They will give up the chase toward something better and try to appreciate how good things are, even at their worst, in this particular right now.

ACKNOWLEDGEMENTS

Thank you to the Creator Institute and Eric Koester who have opened this opportunity for those of us looking for a space to find our message and ourselves. I also want to thank Emily Sparkes, Pea Richelle White, and Faiqa Zafar for being such thoughtful and encouraging editors. You all put the wind in my sails when I thought this was a bunch of gibberish. And thank you to Jordan Green, my fellow author who kept me sane through deadlines.

To my parents who have trusted me more than I have ever trusted myself and have given the most beautiful and searing advice with their off-the-cuff comments. I am proud to be yours.

To Collin, Carrick, Tara, Tatum, and Chris, the siblings that shaped my life through laughter.

To my grandpa, who has been more excited for this book than I have and has offered thoughtful insight and encouragement over phone calls, emails, and mailed articles.

To my wide brood of Cullens, from Mere to her great-grandchildren, from second- to third-cousins. Hearing stories about people from the past has made me want to write stories.

To my beta readers, the people I trusted with the raw words: Caroline Tan, Laura Nejako, Vasudha Kashyap, TJ Gallagher, and Luke Pinto.

To Luke. My silk and steel. There are no right or wrong choices, but if I had to do everything again, existential crises and all, I would do it all again to land back where I am with you.

A huge thank you to my Author Community that sponsored this book and made it a book. One asterisk indicates my paperback buyers, two asterisks indicate that they bought more than one book! Suckers!

But seriously, thank you. This book wouldn't have happened without this support.

Luke Pinto**
Kara Riehl*
Emily Pinto*
Bridget Cullen*
Lucy Gatanis*
William "Bill" Reeves**
Will Cullen**
Molly Shunney
Frank Canavan*
Maggy McCarthy*
Austin Wentzel**
Kelly Cullen*
Aileen Cullen*
Brenda Cullen**
Jenny Becker*
Emily Paulus*

Claire Cullen Hanley*
Anne Cullen Fenwick*
Sam Cullen**
Tim McElroy*
Caroline Tan*
Cecilia Covert*
Amanda Dreyer
Maddie Cullen*
Nora Dolan*
Claire Siemietkowski*
Colby Stackhouse*
Laura Fetters*
Eva Scherer*
Carlie Campbell*
Colleen Canavan**
Katie Ward*

Akhil Pothana
Katherine Iannuzzelli*
Natalie Lynch*
Connor Gallen*
Sean Maloney
Ava Baker*
Seth McMillan*
Adam Levine*
Peggy Hamilton*
Emma Kirby*
Maggie Cullen*
Danny Swift*
Sarah Williams*
Elena MacCartee*
Kim Pinto*
James Kaltman
Burton O. Witthuhn
Nicole Hennessey*
Nakul Grover*
Jessica Pinto*
Reilly Talbot*
Kevin Bannon*
Heather Hernandez*
Kelly Mitstifer*
Olivia Marin*
Zach Zellhart*
Steve Maloney*
Matt Roskin*
Ellen Gosnell*
Quinn O'Connor*
Erica Maddox
Marty Lazzaro*

Claire Pinto*
Kayla Burakovsky*
Colleen Mesler*
Ellen Jordan Cullen*
Alexandra O'Connor
Leo Walsh*
Laura Nejako*
Jason & Liz Whitehead**
Caroline Laubach
Catherine Seher*
Hailey DePreta*
Emma Ortlieb*
Eric Koester*
Annie O'Conor*
Maddie Miller*
Anna Swift*
Maggie Dempsey*
Steve Kelly**
Ron W. Christman*
Traci O'Connor*
Gina Sirianni
Amanda Pierce*
Chris Cullen*
Jack Mullally*
Megan Berryman*
Amanda Cionci
Shane Robinson*
Matt Schaefer*
Marie Sloan Quercetti*
Samantha Grillo*
Sydney Vlasach
Susie Harding*

Tucker Jones*

Joe Brito

Lauren Henning

Emily Daly*

Erin Gilday*

Rachel Arndt**

Emily Daly*

Erin Gilday*

Rachel Arndt**

Kiran Pandey*

Vasudha Kashyap**

Julie Greiner

Kellie Hahn*

Clare Dempsey*

Allie Shwalb*

Marena Casey

Sam Knapp*

Caitlin Moran*

Hilary Hooper*

Stephen Jackson*

Lee Moyer*

Margaret Ling

Alex Bilger*

Alex Kirshenbaum*

Nick Weiss

Sofia Ameti*

Casey Dexter*

Ryan Wall*

Devi Kapo

Collin Jamieson*

John Stinely

JD Costantini*

Keelyn Leonard

Emily Hein

Mike D'Avella

Dani Fruehan

Nick Arndt*

Mike D'Avella

Dani Fruehan

Nick Arndt*

Courtney Testa*

Beth Colarossi**

Melina McLean Duffett

Kate England

Tim and Erika Cullen*

Austin White*

Carly Pendergast*

Alison Barrett*

Caroline Gray

Catie Grant*

Alison Baldwin*

Corena Govan*

Amanda Snook*

Marisa Boyle*

Alana Doyle*

Moira Hamilton*

Paul Kellermann*

Thomas M. Cullen

Courtney Rome*

Anna Duemler*

Lauren Athey*

Cory Murray*

Katherine Goetz*
Rachael Hobbs*
Isabella Isacco*
Kiera Kunkle*
Kristen Solt*
Terry Cullen*
Conor Cullen**
Emily Cullen Santry*
Collin DeMatt*
Brein Cummings*
Kayla Fish*
Lexi Notrica*
Katie Krivda*
John Brzozowski
Rusty Bizaro
Abby Rothwell
Aubree Biggs*
Collin "Heywood" Cullen**
Hannah Semmes
Brian Failor*
Dina M Liberatore
Kristen Hennessey Clarke*
Michael Brown*
Clare Philbin
Kaely Harding*
Aidan Kenney
Julia Born*
Caroline Clarke*
Jake Darley*
Amy Kriebel Portzline*
Amy McNamer

Hailey Quinn*
Jess Frezza*
Mariajose Munoz*
Julia Clarke
Caroline Cullen Barker*
Megan O'Leary
Maria Olsen*
Pauline Collamore*
Colton Richards*
Kathleen "KTB" English*
Gene Ford**
Rosemary Joaquin*
Nora O'Neill*
TJ Gallagher*
Abigail Spires*
Natalia Oliveira
Lilly Deerin*
Mary Ellen Dolan*
Peter Haley*
Julia Dewit
Rosie Walsh*
Maura Cullen Seher*
Laura Wagner*
Rachel Doig*
Alex Vasques**
Taylor Kantner*
Bella Vagnoni*
Zach Pinto*
Jack Carlidge*
Caroline Hannapel*
Tim & Liz Cullen**

Lacey Matan*
Matt Grassucci*
Mary Cullen-Roe*
Yardyn Shraga*
Michael Zielinski*
Mary Joaquin
Jimmy Ronan*
Betty Lou McQuade*
Alex Loffredo*
Tracy Grant*
Erin Mierzwa*
Joan Stamatakis*

Morgan Updyke*
Barb & Owen Byer**
James Wilhelmi*
Bianca Stelian
Alexandra Wald
Patrick Lynch**
Cydney Hamilton*
Zoe Adler*
Mark Western*
Ellen Dugan*
Andrea Brown

APPENDIX

INTRODUCTION

Curran, Thomas and Andrew P. Hill. "How Perfectionism Became a Hidden Epidemic among Young People." *The Conversation.* January 3, 2018.

Gaynor, Keith. "Why Perfectionists Become Depressed | Dr Keith Gaynor." Aware. YouTube, November 14, 2017.

Gilbert, Elizabeth. "No. 4: Studio Visit with Elizabeth Gilbert." Interview by Suleika Jaouad. *Isolation Journals*, November 8, 2020. Video.

Hoffower, Hillary, and Allana Akhtar. "Lonely, Burned Out, and Depressed: The State of Millennials' Mental Health in 2020." Business Insider, October 10, 2020.

Horowitz, Juliana Menasce, and Nikki Graf. "Most U.S. Teens See Anxiety and Depression as a Major Problem Among Their Peers." Pew Research Center, February 19, 2020.

Pope, Daniel. Personal Interview. November 3, 2020.

CHAPTER 1: THE POP QUIZ

Aschwanden, Christie. "Perfectionism Is Killing Us." *Vox*, December 5, 2019.

Gaynor, Dr. Keith. "Why Perfectionists Become Depressed | Dr Keith Gaynor." Aware, YouTube. Accessed May 11, 2021.

Hewitt, Paul, Gordon Flett, Wendy Turnbull-Donovan, and Samuel E Mikail. "The Multidimensional Perfectionism Scale: Reliability, Validity, and Psychometric Properties in Psychiatric Samples." *Psychological Assessment: A Journal of Consulting and Clinical Psychology*, Vol. 3, No. 3.464–468. American Psychological Association. 1991.

"Perfectionism." *Psychology Today*. Accessed February 19, 2021.

"ReSET: Perfectionism." James Madison University. Web page. Accessed February 19, 2021.

Scott, Elizabeth, MS. "Perfectionist Traits: Do These Sound Familiar?" VeryWellMind, February 22, 2020. Accessed February 19, 2021.

CHAPTER 2: THE PERFECTIONISM PENDULUM

Berkheimer, Joy, LMFT. Personal Interview. February 22, 2021.

Brown, Brené. *The Gifts of Imperfection*. Center City, Minnesota, Hazelden Publishing, 2010.

Gherleter, Adam. Personal Interview. December 21, 2021.

Harfoush, Rahaf. "How Burnout Makes Us Less Creative." TED-Talk, The Way We Work, December 2019.

Petersen, Anne Helen. *Can't Even: How Millennials Are Becoming the Burnout Generation.* New York: Houghton Mifflin Harcourt, 2020.

CHAPTER 3: THE INKY FINGER THEORY

Baker, Ava. Personal Interview. November 5, 2020.

Coscarelli, Joe. "Billie Eilish Is Not Your Typical 17-Year-Old Pop Star. Get Used to Her." *New York Times,* March 28, 2019.

Coscarelli, Joe. "How Pop Music Fandom Became Sports, Politics, Religion and All-Out War." *New York Times,* December 25, 2020.

Coscarelli, Joe, and Alicia DeSantis, Antonio de Luca, Alexandra Eaton, Kevin Oliver, Eden Weingart. "How Billie Eilish Is Redefining Teen-Pop Stardom." *New York Times*, April 1, 2019. Video.

Poehler, Amy. *Yes, Please.* New York: First Dey Street. 2014.

The Late Late Show with James Corden. "Billie Eilish Carpool Karaoke." YouTube, Dec 20, 2019.

Weiner, Jonah. 'How Billie Eilish Rode Teenage Weirdness to Stardom.' *New York Times Magazine,* March 11, 2020.

Vanity *Fair*. "Billie Eilish: Same Interview, The Third Year | Vanity Fair." YouTube, November 25, 2019.

CHAPTER 4: THE HAMILTON ETHOS

Brantley, Ben. "Review: *Hamilton*. Young Rebels Changing History and Theater." *The New York Times*, August 6, 2015.

BroadwayWorld. *Hamilton*. Grosses. Last modified March 8, 2020.

BroadwayWorld. *Phantom of the Opera*. Grosses. Last modified March 8, 2020.

BroadwayWorld. *Wicked*. Grosses. Last modified March 8, 2020.

Curran, Thomas. "Our Dangerous Obsession with Perfectionism Is Getting Worse." Filmed November 2018 at TEDMED. Video.

Curran, Thomas and Andrew P. Hill. "How Perfectionism Became a Hidden Epidemic among Young People." *The Conversation*. January 3, 2018.

Fischer, Delanie. Personal Interview. November 16, 2020.

Gerard, Jeremy. "*Hamilton* Opens on Broadway, Bigger and Better Than Ever—Review." *Deadline*, August 6, 2015.

Green, Adam. "Lin-Manuel Miranda's Groundbreaking Hip-Hop Musical, *Hamilton*, Hits Broadway." *Vogue,* June 24, 2015.

Greenblatt, Leah. "*Hamilton*: EW Stage Review." *Entertainment Weekly*, August 6, 2015.

Huntzinger, Jim. "George Washington's Final Warning About the Loss of American Exceptionalism." Finance Town Hall, March 27, 2018.

Jungle Vlog. "Lin-Manuel Miranda Performs 'Alexander Hamilton' at The White House." YouTube, October 1, 2015.

Ministry127.com. "The Cost of Indecision." Accessed January 24, 2021.

Miranda, Lin-Manuel. "#89: Lin-Manuel Miranda // Part Two." Interview by Gillian Pensavalle and Michael Paul Smith. *The Hamilcast*, August 8, 2017.

Miranda, Lin-Manuel. "Lin-Manuel Miranda: Biography." Website. Accessed January 24, 2021.

Miranda, Lin-Manuel. "Lin-Manuel Miranda Recalls His Nerve-Wracking *Hamilton* Performance for the Obamas." Interview by Jimmy Fallon. YouTube, June 24, 2020. Accessed January 24, 2021.

Oswald, Anjelica. "*Hamilton* Tickets Sell for More than $2,000—Here's How Much Money Broadway's Hottest Musical Is Raking in." *Business Insider*, April 13, 2016.

Pease, Donald E. "American Exceptionalism." Oxford Bibliographies. Last modified June 27, 2018.

Thompson, Derek. "Workism Is Making Americans Miserable." *The Atlantic*, February 24, 2019.

THR Staff. "*Hamilton*: Theater Review." *The Hollywood Reporter,*
August 6, 2015.

CHAPTER 5: THE RAMSAY ROAST
"Gordon Ramsay - IMDb." IMDb. Accessed May 11, 2021.

"*Hell's Kitchen*–Emmy Awards." Television Academy. Accessed
January 27, 2021.

Brown, Brené. "Brené Brown Part 1: Daring Greatly." Interview by
Oprah Winfrey. Oprah's *SuperSoul* Conversations, O Network,
August 7, 2017.

Chopped. Season 27, Episode 12.

Jones, Jamie. "17 Times Gordon Ramsay Roasted the Hell Out of
People on Twitter." *Buzzfeed,* February 16, 2017.

Kantayya, Mellini. *Actor. Writer. Whatever.: Stories on My Rise to
the Top of the Bottom of the Entertainment Industry.* Brooklyn,
NY: Ako Dako Press, 2013.

Kohli, Sonali. "When Cooking Became Competition." *The Atlantic,*
October 2, 2014.

Ramsay, Gordon. "Gordon Ramsay: My Life in Five Dishes." Interview by Emily Thomas. BBC, *The Food Chain.* July 25, 2018.

Ramsay, Matilda "Tilly." "I'm Still Running Far Far Away...." @
tillyramsay. TikTok, March 17, 2021.

Random Memes. "Ratatouille Unreleased British version (meme)." YouTube, December 23, 2020.

Rodman, Dr. Samantha. "How Perfectionism Hurts Your Relationships." Talkspace, October 18, 2017.

Swider, Brian, Dana Harai, Amy P. Breidenthal, Laurens Bujold Steed. "The Pros and Cons of Perfectionism, According to Research." *Harvard Business Review,* December 27, 2018.

Weng, Shensheng. "Why Does It Feel Good to See Someone Fail?" *The Conversation,* January 4, 2019.

CHAPTER 6: THE PERFECT PAIRING

Aspan, Maria, Emma Hinchliffe. "The Pandemic Has Derailed Women's Careers and Livelihoods. Is America Giving up on Them?" *Fortune,* January 29, 2021.

Bell, Laurie C. "Women in Their 20s Shouldn't Feel Bad About Wanting a Boyfriend." *The Atlantic,* March 5, 2013.

Chotiner, Isaac. "Why the Pandemic Is Forcing Women Out of the Workforce." *The New Yorker,* October 23, 2020.

Connley, Courtney. "Nearly 2.2 Million Women Left the Workforce between February and October, According to New Analysis." CNBC, November 10, 2020.

de Botton, Alain. Interviewed by Ira Glass. "Choosing Wrong." *This American Life,* June 24, 2016.

Gogoi, Pallavi. "Stuck-At-Home Moms: The Pandemic's Devastating Toll on Women." *NPR,* October 28, 2020.

Hartley, Gemma. "Women Aren't Nags—We're Just Fed Up." *Harper's Bazaar,* September 27, 2017.

Kashen, Julie, Sarah Jane Glynn, Amanda Novello. "How COVID-19 Sent Women's Workforce Progress Backward." Center for American Progress, October 30, 2020.

Kendall, Mikki. *Hood Feminism: Notes from the Women That A Movement Forgot.* New York: Penguin Books, 2021.

Mom (Brenda Cullen). Personal Interview. June 5, 2021.

Ohnesorge, Lauren. "COVID Forced Women Out of the Workforce. Will Their Jobs Still Be There When They Return?" *Triangle Business Journal* in BizWomen, January 29, 2021.

Tolentino, Jia. "Always Be Optimizing" in *Trick Mirror.* New York: Random House, 2019.

"Women in the Workplace: 2020." Lean In, McKinsey & Company, 2020.

CHAPTER 7: THE FUNNY GIRLS

"Any Good Female Comedians That Don't Only Rely on Sex Jokes and Talking Trash?" Reddit. Accessed February 26, 2021.

"List of original Netflix specials."

"London Hughes: To Catch a D*ck | Official Trailer | Netflix." You-Tube, *Netflix,* December 11, 2020.

"Iliza Shlesinger: Freezing Hot | Official Trailer [HD] | Netflix." YouTube, *Netflix,* January 14, 2015.

Grobar, Matt. "'Forever 31' Creator Iliza Shlesinger Talks Opportunities for Comedians in the Digital Arena." *Deadline,* June 12, 2017.

Joaquim, Tanael. "Imperfect Comedy in an Age of Perfection." *Quillette,* May 2, 2019.

Jung, E. Alex. "Wherefore Art Thou, Penis?: Jacqueline Novak on Her Lyrical, Epic Deconstruction of the Blow Job in Get on Your Knees." *Vulture,* September 6, 2019.

Patel, Kasha. Personal Interview. December 11, 2020.

Siemietkowsi, Claire. Personal Interview. November 5, 2020.

Tomlinson, Taylor. "Taylor Tomlinson: Quarter-Life Crisis | Netflix Standup Comedy Special | Trailer." YouTube, *Netflix,* February 20, 2020.

Wood, Jr., Roy. "Phoebe and Roy Wood, Jr. Bomb Their *Daily Show* Auditions." *Sooo Many White Guys,* WNYC, March 26, 2019.

Wright, Megh. "Iliza Shlesinger Came After Other Female Comics, and It Did Not Go Well." *Vulture,* June 16, 2017.

Zinoman, Jacob. "Introducing a Major New Voice in Comedy (Who Also Attacks Comedy)." *New York Times,* March 19, 2018.

CHAPTER 8: THE CITY BLUEPRINT

@peachbaskets. Instagram. Accessed June 18, 2021.

Davis, Nicole. "Could the Next Brooklyn Be Pittsburgh?" *Brooklyn Based,* April 24, 2015.

Florida, Richard. "Class-Divided Cities: New York Edition: Examining America's Dramatic Socio-Economic Residential Segregation." *Bloomberg CityLab,* January 24, 2013.

Florida, Richard. "The Rise of the Creative Class." *Washington Monthly,* May 2002.

Jay, Meg. "Why 30 Is Not the New 20." TED. Web page. Accessed May 31, 2021.

Khazan, Olga. "The Problem with Being Perfect." *The Atlantic,* November 5, 2018.

Maslin, Janet. "Bohemian Soul Mates in Obscurity." *The New York Times,* January 17, 2010.

Odell, Jenny. *How to Do Nothing: Resisting the Attention Economy.* Brooklyn, NY: Melville House. 2019.

Petersen, Anne Helen. "How Millennials Became the Burnout Generation." Buzzfeed, January 5, 2019.

Plitt, Amy and Raven Snook. "Should You Move to New York City?" *Curbed,* December 26, 2019.

Walsh, Leo. Personal Interview. April 14, 2021.

CHAPTER 9: THE POUR

"Press Pause: "Friends," Party Games, and Classic Cocktails Recipes." theSkimm, April 13, 2020. Accessed on February 11, 2021.

"Press Pause: The Best of 2020." theSkimm, December 28, 2020. Accessed on February 11, 2021.

"Treat Yo Self–Parks and Recreation." Parks and Recreation, YouTube, June 22, 2018.

"What You Need to Know Today about the Coronavirus." Associated Press, April 13, 2020. Accessed on February 11, 2021.

Borges, Anna. "30 Self-Care Tips That Are So Extra They Just Might Work." *Buzzfeed*, March 26, 2017.

Cheyenne, Yasmine. "How to Balance Activism and Self-Care, According to a Wellness Coach." Interview by Eliza Dumais, Refinery29, July 14, 2020.

Copeland, Blythe. "Rainy Weather Brought a Cozy Vibe to This Washington, D.C., Micro Wedding." *Martha Stewart Weddings,* February 16, 2021.

Harris, Aisha. "The history of self-care." *Slate.*

Mason, Maggie and Robin McDowell. "Palm Oil Labor Abuses Linked to World's Top Brands, Banks." *The Associated Press*, September 24, 2020.

Ortiz, Robin and Lauren Sinko. "Responding to the Trauma of COVID-19: Individual and Community Actions." U Penn. July 2, 2020.

Petzrela, Natalia Mehrlman. "When Wellness Was Weird." Well + Good, July 14, 2015.

Pullmann, Erin. "The 21 Best Subscription Boxes for Women—2021 Readers' Choice Awards." *My Subscription Addiction*, January 14, 2020. Last updated February 14, 2021.

Quinn, Daley. "Self-Care Is a Lifeline for Many Women—But It's Not Enough." Well + Good, September 4, 2019.

Ramos, Alisha. "We Planned Your Weekend for You." Issue #183, "Girls Night In," August 31, 2020. Accessed on February 11, 2021.

Smith, Amanda, LCSW. "Intentional Self-Care." Blog.

Tucker, Phebe, MD and Christopher S. Czapla, MD. "Post-COVID Stress Disorder: Another Emerging Consequence of the Global Pandemic." *Psychiatric Times*, January 8, 2021.

Zalben, Alex. "Here's Why Nobody Can Get into the Good Place on 'The Good Place.'" *Decider*, January 10, 2019.

CHAPTER 10: CREATIVITY INCORPORATED

"Comedic Arts | Emerson College." Emerson College. Accessed on February 27, 2021.

"Comedy Writing and Performance." Columbia College Chicago. Accessed on February 27, 2021.

"David Rogier, MBA '11, CEO & Co-Founder of MasterClass." YouTube, Stanford Graduate School of Business. Accessed on February 27, 2021.

"Masterclass Home Page." Masterclass. Accessed on February 27, 2021.

"MFA Programs Database." *Poets & Writers*. Accessed on February 27, 2021.

"Minor in Comedy Writing." New York University, Tisch School of the Arts. Accessed on February 27, 2021.

"When Everyone's Super..." YouTube, TheBlindSpot. Accessed on February 27, 2021.

Bourne, Michael. "MFA Programs in the Time of COVID-19: Writers, Teachers, and Administrators Plan for a New Normal." *Poets & Writers*, Sept/Oct 2020.

Díaz, Junot. "MFA v. POC." *The New Yorker*, April 14, 2014.

Gilbert, Elizabeth. *Big Magic*. New York: Riverhead Books. 2015.

Keane, Sean. "The Best Actors and Comedians Who Came through UCB." *Yardbarker*, June 4, 2018.

Kleon, Austin. Personal Interview. November 9, 2020.

O'Neil, Luke. "Could a College Degree in Comedy Be Anything Other Than a Joke?" *New York Times*, June 13, 2016.

Raftery, Brian. "And... Scene." *New York Magazine*, September 23, 2011.

Tan, Megan. "Living a Life with No Ceiling | Megan Tan | TEDx-Dirigo." TEDx Talks, YouTube. December 6, 2016.

CHAPTER 11: THE HAPPY GIRLS

@blackatdcprivs. "As Soon as I Came to Visitation I Was Only Really Welcomed by Other Students of My Own Race (African American)." Instagram, August 11, 2020.

Curran, Thomas. "Thomas Curran: How Can We Teach Kids to Accept Imperfection?" Interview by MANOUSH ZOMORODI. *NPR. September 20, 2019.*

Georgetown Visitation. "Catherine Paul '09." Georgetown Visitation, "Visitation Voices" series. Accessed March 3, 2021.

Georgetown Visitation, "Financials-Georgetown Visitation." Georgetown Visitation, Annual Financial Report, 2018-2019. (pw: visigratitude)

Georgetown Visitation, "Joella '22." Georgetown Visitation, "Visitation Voices" series. Accessed March 3, 2021.

Georgetown Visitation, "Katrina Fludd '04." Georgetown Visitation, "Visitation Voices" series. Accessed March 3, 2021.

Georgetown Visitation, "Maggie Rose '06 (Margaret Durante)." Georgetown Visitation, "Visitation Voices" series. Accessed March 3, 2021.

Georgetown Visitation, "Peggy Judge Hamilton, '85." Georgetown Visitation, "Visitation Voices" series. Accessed May 18, 2021.

Georgetown Visitation, "Sr. Sylvie-Marie." Georgetown Visitation, "Visitation Voices" series. Accessed May 18, 2021.

Georgetown Visitation, "Tuition, Financial Aid & Scholarships." Georgetown Visitation. Accessed March 13, 2021.

Gross-Loh, Christine. "The Never-Ending Controversy Over All-Girls Education." *The Atlantic,* March 20, 2014.

Hamilton, Peggy Judge. Personal Interview. March 1, 2021.

Ward, Katie, Caroline Laubach, Amanda Pierce, Nora Dolan, and Hailey DePreta. Personal Interview. February 28, 2021.